Helen F. Ormiston

The ideal cook book

Helen F. Ormiston
The ideal cook book
ISBN/EAN: 9783744785853
Printed in Europe, USA, Canada, Australia, Japan
Cover: Foto ©Lupo / pixelio.de

More available books at **www.hansebooks.com**

COMPILED AND EDITED BY A COMMITTEE OF LADIES
IN THE INTEREST OF CHRISTIAN WORK

"With baked, and broiled, and stewed, and toasted,
And fried, and boiled, and smoked, and roasted,
We treat the town."

NEW YORK
1889

COPYRIGHT, 1889, BY
T. W. ORMISTON.

Press of J. J. Little & Co.,
Astor Place, New York.

> "Some hae meat that canna eat,
> And some could eat that want it;
> But we hae meat and we can eat,
> Sae let the Lord be thankit."

CONTENTS.

SOUPS.

	PAGE		PAGE
Bean Soup	9	Mock Bisque Soup	7
Bisque of Lobster	9	Noodles for Soup	11
Bouillon	5	Ox-tail Soup	8
Cream Chicken Soup	6	Oyster Soup	10
Chicken Soup	7	Oyster Stew	10
Cream Soup	6	Purée of Salmon	10
Corn Soup	9	Purée of Peas	6
Egg Balls for Soup	11	Tomato Soup	8
Giblet Soup	7		

FISH.

Blue fish, baked	14	Halibut Steak	14
Chowder, fish	15	Lobster, deviled	18
Clam Fritters	19	Lobster Pâtés	18
Clams, deviled	17	Lobsters, to boil	19
Codfish, boiled	13	Oysters, escalloped	16
Codfish, fried in Butter	16	Oysters, creamed	16
Codfish, picked-up	16	Oysters à la Poulette	17
Codfish Balls	16	Oysters, pickled	17
Crabs, deviled	18	Shad, boiled	15
Crabs, to boil	19	Shad, baked	14
Crabs, soft shell	18	Trout, baked	14
Fish, escalloped	15		

POULTRY.

Chicken Fricassee	22	Duck, cold, to use up	25
Chicken, smothered	22	Goose, roast	24
Chicken Pâtés	23	Pigeons, stewed	25
Chicken Pie	23	Squabs, broiled	25
Chicken, boned	23	Squabs, roast	26
Chicken Croquettes	24	Turkey, roast	21
Duck, roast	24	Turkey, ragoût of	22

MEATS.

	PAGE		PAGE
Beef, roast	27	Mutton, roast	30
Beef, roast with Yorkshire Pudding	27	Mutton, boiled	30
Beef, stewed with Mushrooms	27	Mutton Chops and Tomato purée	30
Beef, cannelon of	28	Pork, roast leg of	35
Beefsteak, broiled	28	Spare-rib, roast	36
Beefsteak and Onions	28	Sweetbreads	35
Beef's Heart	29	Sweetbreads, brown fricassee of	35
Beef (corned), pressed	29	Veal, roast	32
Ham, boiled	36	Veal Scallop	33
Ham and Eggs	36	Veal, cannelon of	33
Kidney Stew	29	Veal Cutlets	34
Lamb, roast	31	Veal Croquettes	34
Lamb Chops	31	Veal Loaf	32
Lamb, stewed with Mushroom Sauce	31	Veal Pot-Pie with Dumplings	32

GAME.

Grouse, roasted with Bacon	38	Rabbit, fricasseed	73
Partridge	39	Venison, haunch of	37
Pigeon, stewed	38		

SAUCES FOR MEAT AND FISH.

Apple Sauce	44	Gravy for Turkey	42
Bread Sauce	41	Horse-radish Sauce	42
Bread Sauce for Partridge and Grouse	41	Mint Sauce	43
		Oyster Sauce	42
Caper Sauce	41	Oyster Dressing	44
Cranberry Jelly	44	Sauce for Salmon and other Fish	43
Drawn Butter	42		
Dressing for Fowls	44	Sauce for Cod and other Fish	42
Gravy for Roast Meats	42	Tomato Sauce	43

EGGS.

Eggs, boiled	45	Eggs, poached	45
Eggs, baked	45	Eggs, escalloped	46
Egg Basket	46	Eggs, scrambled	45
Eggs, creamed	46	Omelet	47

CONTENTS.

SALADS.

	PAGE		PAGE
Cabbage Salad, boiled Dressing for	51	Lobster Salad without Oil	49
		Mayonnaise Dressing	50
Chicken Salad	50	Potato Salad	50
Lobster Salad	49	Salad Dressing	49

VEGETABLES.

Asparagus	57	Potato Croquettes	54
Beans, Boston baked	58	Potatoes, escalloped	54
Beans, string	57	Potato Puff	54
Celery, stewed	57	Potatoes, warmed-up	54
Egg Plant	55	Potatoes, lyonnaise	55
Egg Plant, Miss F.'s	56	Potatoes, Saratoga Fried	55
Macaroni, baked	58	Potatoes, sweet	55
Macaroni and Tomatoes	59	Rice, boiled	60
Parsnips	57	Rice Croquettes	59
Pease	58	Salsify or Oyster Plant	55
Potatoes, boiled	53	Tomatoes, stewed	56
Potatoes, chopped, baked	53	Tomatoes, escalloped	57

BREAD.

Biscuit, Baking Powder	65	Griddle Cakes, wheat	66
Bread	61	Hominy	68
Bread, Boston brown	63	Muffins	65
Bread, brown	64	Mush, boiled	68
Bread, graham	62	Oatmeal Porridge	67
Bread, white	61	Pop Overs	65
Corn Cake	66	Rolls, Parker House	63
Gems, graham	65	Rolls, raised graham	64
Gems, wheat	65	Waffles	66
Griddle Cakes, buckwheat	67	Wheaten Grits	68

WEIGHTS AND MEASURES.

CAKES.

Almond Cake	73	Bread Cake	72
Angel's Cake	74	Cake without Eggs	74
Boiled Frosting	78	Chocolate Cake	72

CONTENTS.

	PAGE		PAGE
Chocolate Caramel	76	Ginger Wafers	76
Cocoanut	77	Gold Cake	72
Cocoanut Cake	73	Hermit's	76
Coffee Cake	73	Hickory Nut Cake	71
Cookies	75	Hints for Making Cake	71
Corn Starch Cake	75	Icing	77
Cream Custard	77	Jelly Cake	78
Cream Fruit Cake	73	Layer Cake	73
Cream Sponge Cake	72	Lemon Filling	77
Crullers	76	Minnehaha Cake	75
Doughnuts	76	Raisin	77
Easy Frosting	78	Silver Cake	72
Fig Filling	77	Sour Cream	77
Fruit Cake	74	Sponge Cake	74
Gingerbread	75	White Cake	71

PIES.

	PAGE		PAGE
Apple Pie	79	Méringue Custard Pie	81
Cocoanut Pie	80	Mince Meat	81
Cream Pie	80	Pie-plant Pie	80
Custard Pie	81	Plain Pastry for One Pie	79
Lemon Méringue Pie	80	Puff Pastry	79
Lemon Pie	79	Pumpkin Pie	80

PUDDINGS AND SAUCES.

	PAGE		PAGE
Apple Pudding	85	Lemon Sauce	89
Batter Pudding	86	Minute Pudding	86
Boiled Lemon Pudding	87	Peach Pudding	87
Cocoanut Pudding	86	Pudding Sauce	89
Cottage Pudding	84	Queen of Puddings	84
Cream Sauce	88	Rice Pudding	84
English Plum Pudding	86	Roly-Poly	86
Fairy Butter	88	Sour Sauce	89
Fig Pudding	88	Steamed Cabinet Pudding	85
Foam Sauce	88	Steamed Pudding	83
General Directions	83	Strawberry Short-Cake	88
Graham Pudding	83	Suet Pudding	85
Hard Sauce	89	White Steamed Pudding	85
Indian Pudding	84		

CONTENTS. ix

FANCY DESSERTS.

	PAGE		PAGE
Baked Cup Custards	96	Lemon and Fruit Jelly	93
Blanc Mange	94	Lemon Jelly	93
Boiled Custard	96	Orange Float	92
Charlotte Russe	94	Orange Jelly	93
Charlotte Russe	94	Orange Soufflé	92
Chocolate Blanc Mange	95	Plain Corn Starch Pudding	95
Coffee Jelly	92	Prune Jelly	96
Crême de Thyra	97	Rice Snow	92
Dessert	97	Rock Cream	91
Farina Jelly	94	Snow Pudding	91
Floating Island	95	Spanish Cream	93
Ice Cream	98	Tapioca Cream	91
Imperial Granum Ice Cream	98	Tarte d'Elysee	97

BEVERAGES.

A Summer Drink	102	Coffee	101
Chocolate	102	Communion Wine	102
Cocoa	102	Tea	101

JELLIES AND PRESERVES.

Baked Apples	104	Grape Preserves	103
Crab Apple Jelly	104	Peaches	103
Currant Jelly	103	Strawberry Jam	104

THE SICK-ROOM.

Beef Tea	118	Indian Meal Gruel	120
Beef Tea	118	Kumyss	120
Beef Tea	118	Lemon Drink	120
Beef Juice	119	Mustard Plasters	121
Chicken Broth	119	Mutton Broth	119
Clam Broth	119	Sago Gruel	119
Cough Syrup	121	Scraped Beef	118
Flaxseed Lemonade	120	Toast Water	120
Flaxseed Tea	120		

DIRECTIONS FOR SETTING A TABLE AND SERVING A DINNER.

A CANTON-FLANNEL (which should be double-faced, and can be procured at any dry-goods store) is first laid on, and over this the tablecloth, with the centre fold directly in the middle of the table; it is always well to place the chairs so that each seat will come just where it belongs, and there will be no danger of crowding. The host and hostess, or the two heads of the family, should always occupy the seats at either end of the table.

At each place should be laid, at the left, as many forks as there are to be courses, and at the right the knives, and spoon for soup, with the glasses which are necessary; if individual salts are used these are put in the centre, just in front of the place left for the plate; the butter plate is placed at the top of the forks; the napkin, neatly folded, with either a roll or thickly cut piece of bread, is laid in the centre, or if the first course is to be oysters it is placed at the left of the forks; a butter ball on each plate, and each glass filled with water just before the dinner is announced, saves much trouble. On a side table, arranged exactly in the order you intend using them, should be the plates for each course, so that there will be no confusion. A centre-piece of flowers is always an addition to any table, and if one does not wish it, a growing plant which is not too high will answer, as it is never in good taste to have anything which will interfere with the opposite parties seeing each other. Small dishes containing jellies, salted almonds, pickles or olives, and bon-bons are arranged at points where they will look well. The soup ladle is laid in front of the hostess, and the carving knife and fork, resting on knife rests, are at the right and left of the host.

For example, we will give a dinner of six courses, consisting of raw oysters, soup, fish, meat, salad, and dessert. This will require three forks and three knives (two of which should be silver, the fish and salad knife) and a soup spoon at each place, the oyster forks being laid across the plates, which should be on the table before the guests are seated. The attendant will have the plates for the soup, fish, and meat warming; the plates for the salad and dessert will be neatly arranged on a side table (the dessert ones with either spoons or forks, whichever are to be used, also the larger spoon for serving, so that when the plates are placed on the table the accessories will be also); the plates, with the finger bowls and the cups for the after dinner coffee, with a small spoon on each saucer, are also ready.

The dinner is quietly announced without the ringing of a bell. We will imagine the guests seated. The attendant, with a tray in her hand, stands at the left of the hostess. On her tray she immediately passes to the left of each person the pepper. When all are through the plates are removed, not more being carried at once than can be easily managed on the tray.

The soup is then brought in and, with the warmed plates, placed in front of the hostess. As each plate is supplied it is taken, the first being passed to the lady guest at the right or left of the host, the ladies being served first and then the gentlemen; the attendant, going to the left side of the person, places the plate on the table, and so on until each one is served.

It is an excellent plan to have what is called a knife and fork basket, which has two compartments; and, when all are through, the attendant, going to the *right* of each person, removes the spoons from the plates, puts them noiselessly into the basket, and removes them to the pantry. The plates are then taken on the tray, piling easily, and the course of fish is brought and placed before the host. As the fish is served, the potatoes, which are in a dish on a side table, are then passed, each person helping himself. Pickles are usually served, with fish, and are also passed. At a motion from the hostess, the fish is removed and the table again cleared, the knives and forks being put in the basket, knives on one side and the forks on the other, the plates being taken off on a tray.

The roast is placed before the host, and, with its vegetable or vegetables, served in like manner. If jelly is used with this course, it is taken on the plates; but if a sweet pickle (such as peaches, pears, etc.), it is always well to have them prepared in saucers ready to be passed to each guest, and so save all delay. In this case a teaspoon should also have been put at each place. The table is again cleared, and the salad is placed before the *hostess* and passed as before, using crackers with this course instead of bread. After the salad is removed, butter plates, salts, and any knives or forks which have not been used and so left on the table, are then taken off on the tray, and the crumb-tray is brought and all crumbs are removed, either a scraper or brush being used.

The dessert plates, which have been arranged with the necessaries for serving, are placed in front of the hostess, and the dessert is brought on; this is passed as before, then removed.

The small cup of coffee is served, a plate with a finger bowl placed before each guest, and the attendant retires.

This is not too much form for an every-day dinner of three courses, soup, meat and vegetables, and dessert; and the attendant, who daily serves a dinner as it should be, will never be confused with company, as she is simply doing what she is accustomed to for a few more in number.

There should be as little noise as possible, and the understanding between mistress and maid so thorough that a look will be sufficient, and no words necessary.

It is a good plan to have a menu of the dinner pinned up, one in the kitchen and one in the pantry, so that nothing will be forgotten and no mistake occur.

SOUPS.

"Good broth and good keeping do much now and then,
Good diet, with wisdom, best comforteth men."

THE basis of all soup should be uncooked meat. To this may be added cracked bones of cooked meat, of any kind; but for flavor and nourishment depend upon the juices of the meat which was put in raw. Put the meat into cold water, allowing about one and one-half pints for one pound of bone and meat. Let it simmer slowly for six hours at least, only uncovering the pot once in a great while to see if there is danger of the water sinking too rapidly. During the seventh hour, take off the soup, and set away, still closely covered, until next morning. About an hour before dinner take out the bone and meat, remove the fat from the surface of the stock, set the soup over the fire, and add a little salt to bring up the scum, which should be carefully skimmed off. Strain always through a cullender, after which clear soups should be filtered through a hair sieve.

Bouillon.

A knuckle of beef well cracked and a small beef bone, one-half each of a carrot, turnip, and onion, a little celery. Cover the bones with water and let the kettle stand where it will boil slowly all day, twelve hours if possible; the last three hours have the vegetables in. Salt, strain through a cullender into a stone jar. In the morning remove the fat and heat the jelly, which should be solid, and strain through a flannel bag. Bouillon is simply a good strong stock well seasoned.

Cream Chicken Soup.

Boil two chickens till tender, take them up; strain the liquor and add to it two white onions (whole), one carrot, one turnip, and one potato. Let it boil up, strain into a dish, and set aside till cool. Remove all fat and return to the fire. Rub together one large tablespoonful of butter and the same of flour until very light; stir into the liquor and allow it to come to a boil. Have ready a quart of rich milk or cream, pour in, stirring all the time; do not allow it to boil. Serve as hot as possible.

Cream Soup.

Three pounds of lean veal, one onion, one-half pound pearl barley, four quarts water, salt, pepper, and a cup of milk. Cut the veal and onion very small, put on with the barley. Boil slowly until reduced to two quarts. Strain, rubbing the barley through a sieve. Season with pepper and salt, simmer three minutes. It should be white and thick as cream, when you have added the cup of boiling milk, after which it should not boil.

Purée of Peas.

One pint of split peas soaked over night, three small onions, three stalks celery, two small carrots, one bunch of sweet herbs, one pint tomatoes, three tablespoonfuls of butter rolled in flour, three quarts of water, and pepper and salt to taste. Put all on to cook together except tomatoes and butter. The vegetables must be chopped fine; stew steadily and gently three hours. Rub to a purée through a sieve, and put in the tomatoes freed of bits of skin and cores, and cut into bits. Season and return to the fire to cook for twenty minutes. longer, closely covered; stir in the butter divided into teaspoonfuls, each rolled in flour. Boil up and serve; dice of fried bread should be put into the tureen.

Chicken Soup.

Take the fat from the top of the liquor in which a chicken has been boiled, and put on the soup to heat. Meanwhile boil half a cupful of rice tender in a pint of salted milk, and when the rice is soft stir in a teaspoonful of butter, worked up in flour to prevent oiling; when the soup boils clear, skim and add the rice and milk, with two tablespoonfuls of minced parsley. Pepper and salt to taste; simmer ten minutes. Chop up three hard-boiled eggs fine; put into the tureen and pour the soup upon them.

Giblet Soup.

Break up the skeleton of a roast chicken. Put bones, stuffing, and giblets into a soup-kettle with four quarts of water. Boil one hour and take out the giblets. Boil the rest an hour longer; strain, cool, and skim. Then put back over the fire to simmer. Meanwhile you should have fried an onion (sliced) in two tablespoonfuls of butter; then taking out the onion have stirred in a *great* spoonful of browned flour, and cooked it, stirring incessantly five minutes. Now thin this mixture with a few spoonfuls of your soup, and strain into soup-kettle. Add the chopped giblets; season well, and serve hot.

Mock Bisque Soup.

Stew a can of tomatoes, and strain them. Add a pinch of baking soda to remove the acid. In another sauce-pan boil three pints of milk; thicken with a tablespoonful of corn starch previously mixed with a little cold milk. Add a lump of butter the size of an egg. Salt and pepper to taste, and mix with the tomatoes. Let all come to a boil and serve at once, *very hot.*

Tomato Soup.

Skin carefully one quart of ripe tomatoes, put them in soup-pot, pour over two quarts of rich soup stock. Let simmer an hour, run through a sieve, return to the pot, season with pepper, salt, and pieces of butter rolled in flour, and a cup of boiling milk. Let it come to a boil, and serve at once.

Tomato Soup.

Open a can of tomatoes, and cut them up small. Take the fat from the top of the liquor in which a leg of mutton has been boiled, put over the fire with the tomatoes and half a cup of raw rice, and cook slowly one hour. Season to taste; adding a lump of loaf sugar, and a tablespoonful of butter rolled in flour; simmer five minutes, and pour into the tureen.

Ox-tail Soup.

One ox-tail, two pounds of lean beef, four carrots, three onions, thyme and parsley, and pepper and salt to taste; two tablespoonfuls of browned flour, four quarts of cold water. Cut the tail into joints and fry brown in good dripping. Slice the onions and two carrots, and fry in the same, when you have taken out the pieces of tail. When done tie them, with thyme and parsley, in a lace bag and drop into the soup-kettle. Put in the tail, then the beef cut into strips. Grate over them the two whole carrots, pour over all the water, and boil slowly four hours. Strain and season; thicken with brown flour wet with cold water; boil fifteen minutes longer and serve.

Corn Soup.

One can of sweet corn, one quart of boiling water, one quart of milk, three tablespoonfuls of butter rolled in one of flour; two eggs, pepper and salt, one tablespoonful tomato catsup. Drain the corn and chop fine. Put on in the boiling water and cook one hour. Rub through a cullender, leaving the husks behind, and return it with the water in which it has boiled to the fire. Season, boil gently five minutes, and stir in the butter and flour. Have ready the boiling milk, pour it upon the beaten eggs and then into the soup. Simmer one minute, stirring all the while; take up, add the catsup, and serve.

Bean Soup.

Soak a quart of dried beans all night in cold water, throw this off next morning and cover with water a little more than lukewarm. Put over the fire with five quarts of cold water and one pound of salt pork. A bone of veal or beef may be added, if you have it. Boil slowly for at least four hours: shred into it a small onion, four stalks of celery and pepper— the pork may salt it sufficiently: simmer half an hour longer; rub through a cullender until only husks and fibres remain, and send to table hot.

Bisque of Lobster.

Meat of one boiled lobster, or a can of preserved lobster, one quart of milk, one quart of boiling water, one-half cup of rolled crackers, four tablespoonfuls of butter, cayenne pepper and salt. Pound the coral and other soft parts of the lobster to a paste, and simmer five minutes in the boiling water. Cut the rest of the lobster meat into dice and put into a saucepan with the cracker crumbs. Pour the red water over them and heat to a boil, when add pepper, salt, and butter. Simmer, covered, half an hour, taking care it does not scorch. Heat the milk with a pinch of soda in another vessel, and after the lobster is in the tureen pour this in boiling hot. Pass sliced lemon with it.

Oyster Soup.

Put one hundred oysters and liquor together into a saucepan; when the oysters begin to curl up, lift out of juice with strainer. When the liquor comes to a boil, add two large tablespoonfuls of butter rubbed together with one and a half tablespoonfuls of flour. Let this boil, put in a pinch of cayenne pepper, half teaspoonful ground mace. Add one quart and one-half pint of milk, and stir until it comes to a boil, then drop in the oysters. Have in the soup tureen the whites of two eggs well beaten and three crackers rolled very fine.

Oyster Stew.

For each stew required place in your saucepan from twelve to eighteen fresh plump oysters, *free from any of their liquor;* add a little salt, pepper, and a small lump of sweet butter; pour on a half cup of boiling water, set over a brisk fire, and bring to a boil; then add half or three-fourths of a cup of rich sweet milk, bring to a boil again, take off immediately, and serve at once.

Purée of Salmon.

Open a small can of salmon and remove all bone, skin, oil, etc. Mash fine. Put over, in a double boiler, one quart of milk, one teaspoonful salt, one salt-spoon ground mace, one pinch of red pepper; add one spoonful of butter and one heaping tablespoonful of corn starch dissolved in a cup of cold water; pour this slowly into boiling milk till it thickens. When smooth and thick, put in salmon. Let cook together five minutes and rub through a fine sieve. Put back and bring to a boil, and eat with crisp crackers (which are Boston crackers, split, buttered, and browned in quick oven).

Noodles for Soup.

Beat one egg light, add a pinch of salt, and flour enough to make a stiff dough; roll out in very thin sheets and roll up tightly. Shave off thin slices—put them in the soup and boil ten minutes.

Egg Balls for Soup.

Rub the yolks of three or four hard boiled eggs to a smooth paste, with a *very* little melted butter. To this add two raw ones, beaten light, and enough flour to hold the paste together. Make into balls with floured hands and set in a cold place until just before your soup comes off, when drop in carefully and boil one minute.

FISH.

Nearly all kinds of fish lose their flavor soon after they are taken from the water.

Fish are fresh when the eyes are clear, the fins stiff, the gills red and hard to open.

Before broiling fish rub the gridiron with fat to keep it from sticking. Place the inside of the fish down on the gridiron, and nearly cook before turning; butter the skin before turning towards the fire.

Salt fish should be soaked in cold water over night before cooking.

Boiled Codfish.

Lay the fish in cold water, slightly salted, for half an hour before it is time to cook it, wipe dry and put in a fish kettle with water enough to cover it, in which has been dissolved a little salt. Let it boil quite briskly. A piece of cod weighing three pounds will be cooked in half an hour from the time the water begins to boil. If cooked in a cloth it will require twice as long to boil.

Have ready a sauce prepared thus: To one gill of boiling water add as much milk, and when it is scalding hot stir in two tablespoonfuls of butter,—a little at a time, that it may melt without oiling,—a tablespoonful of flour wet with cold water, and as this thickens, two beaten eggs. Season with salt and chopped parsley, and after one good boil take from the fire and add a dozen capers. Put the fish into a hot dish and pour sauce over it.

Baked Trout.

Dry fish thoroughly inside and out. Sprinkle inside with pepper and salt and put in a small cup of butter; put in dripping-pan on a rack. Just before taking from the oven pour over the fish a cup of sweet cream. Let it brown if necessary; thicken the gravy with a little flour.

Halibut Steak.

Wash and wipe the steaks dry. Beat up two or three eggs, and roll out some Boston or other brittle crackers upon the kneading board, until they are as fine as dust. Dip each steak into beaten egg, then into the cracker crumbs (when you have salted the fish), and fry in hot fat—or you can broil the steak upon a buttered gridiron over a clear fire, first seasoning with salt and pepper. When done lay in a hot dish, butter well, and cover closely.

Baked Shad.

Clean, wash, and wipe the fish, which should be a large one. Make a stuffing of bread crumbs, mixed with butter, salt, and pepper, and sweet herbs; stuff the shad and sew it up. Lay it in the baking pan, with a cupful of water to keep it from burning, and bake an hour, basting with butter and water until it is tender throughout and well browned. Take up and put in a hot dish and cover tightly, while you boil up the gravy with a great spoonful of catsup, a tablespoonful of browned flour which has been wet with cold water, and the juice of a lemon. Garnish with sliced lemon and water-cresses.

Baked Blue Fish.

Grate or chop bread (without the crust), season with pepper, salt, and butter; wash the fish well and cover it with the bread crumbs, put bits of butter over it, and bake in quick oven one hour, basting often.

Boiled Shad.

Clean, wash, and wipe the fish. Sprinkle with salt and wrap in clean linen cloth. Cover with salted water, and boil from half an hour to three-quarters, in proportion to the size. Serve on a hot dish with a boat of drawn butter.

Drawn Butter.

Stir two teaspoons of flour into a heaping tablespoonful of butter ; stir into a cup of boiling milk, add salt to taste, and boil one minute.

Fish Chowder.

Take a fresh fish weighing eight pounds (cod is best), clean well, leaving on the skin, cut in slices one and one-half inches thick : cut one and one-half pounds of fat salt pork in thin slices, do the same with sixteen good-sized potatoes and two onions (if liked). Put the pork in a kettle and fry out all the fat ; remove the pork, leaving the fat, to which add three pints of water ; put in layer of fish, then one of potato and onion ; lay on the pork cut in strips, and sift over one tablespoonful of salt, one teaspoonful of pepper, and a little flour, then more fish, etc. Fill up with water until it covers the whole, put over a good fire, and boil twenty-five minutes. Have ready one quart of boiling milk and a dozen split crackers ; add these, and let all boil together five minutes.

Escalloped Fish.

Take cooked fish, put alternate layers of fish and cream sauce in a baking dish. Cover with fine cracker and pieces of butter. Bake one hour.

Codfish Fried in Butter.

Pull codfish apart and soak over night. In the morning dry thoroughly, make a batter of two eggs and a tablespoon of flour, roll the fish in it, and fry in butter.

Picked-up Codfish.

Put fish on the stove in cold water; keep warm, but do not boil until the fish is softened; remove bones and skin, shred finely and put it in a saucepan, with rich milk, in proportion of one pint of milk to one cup of fish; let come to a boil and thicken with a teaspoonful of flour. Just before taking from the stove, stir in butter the size of an egg, and one egg well beaten. Season with pepper, and garnish with hard-boiled eggs.

Codfish Balls.

One pound of codfish picked fine, two pints raw potatoes cut in small pieces. Boil together in a little water. When done soft, drain and mash; add three eggs, half cup butter, and pepper to taste. Make into balls, and fry in hot lard.

Scalloped Oysters.

Butter a dish that is about three inches deep, put in a layer of crackers and bread crumbs; then a layer of oysters, free from their liquor, then bits of butter; sprinkle with pepper and salt. Do this until you have used a quart of oysters—having the cracker crumbs on top. Over the whole pour a teacupful of sweet cream or rich milk, and bake three-quarters of an hour.

Creamed Oysters.

Fifty shell oysters, one quart sweet cream or rich milk, butter, pepper and salt to taste. Put the cream and oysters in separate kettles to heat; the oysters in their own liquor, and let them come to a boil. When sufficiently cooked, skim, take out of the liquor, and put in a dish to keep warm. Put cream and liquor together, season to taste, and thicken with powdered cracker. When sufficiently thick, stir in the oysters, and serve.

Oysters à la Poulette.

Cook about three dozen good sized oysters, with pepper, nutmeg, and a little butter; drain on a cloth, and save the liquor. Put in a saucepan an ounce of butter with an ounce of flour; cook a little, dilute with part of the oyster liquor and veal broth; boil five minutes, add three egg yolks, two ounces of butter, lemon juice, and a pinch of red pepper; stir, mix well without boiling, and press through a napkin into another saucepan; stir in the oysters to heat, and add chopped parsley; serve at once.

Pickled Oysters.

Take one hundred fresh oysters, scald them in their own liquor, then lay them on a plate to cool; strain liquor, add one pint best white vinegar, one dozen blades of mace, two dozen whole cloves, two dozen whole black peppers, and one large red pepper broken into bits. Boil up fairly, and when oysters are nearly cold, pour over them scalding hot. Cover the jar in which they are, and put away in cool place.

Deviled Clams.

Chop fifty clams very fine, take two tomatoes, one onion, chopped equally fine; a little parsley, thyme, and sweet marjoram, a little salt, pepper, and bread crumbs, adding the juice of the clams until the mixture is the consistency of sausage; put it in the shells, with a lump of butter on each, cover with bread crumbs, and bake one half hour.

Deviled Crabs.

One cup crab meat, picked from shells of well-boiled crabs, two tablespoonfuls fine bread crumbs or rolled cracker, yolks of two hard-boiled eggs chopped, juice of a lemon, one-half teaspoonful of mustard, a little cayenne pepper and salt, one cup good drawn butter. Mix one spoonful crumbs with chopped crab meat, yolks, seasoning, drawn butter. Fill scallop shells—large clam shells will do—or small paté pans—with the mixture; sift crumbs over top, heat to slight browning in quick oven.

Soft Shell Crabs.

Fry in butter or lard.

Deviled Lobster.

One can preserved lobster, three tablespoonfuls butter, four tablespoonfuls vinegar, one-half teaspoonful made mustard, one good pinch cayenne pepper, boiled eggs for garnishing, salt. Empty contents lobster can into bowl one hour before using it. Mince evenly. Put vinegar, butter, and seasoning into saucepan; when it simmers add lobster. Cook slowly, covered, one-half hour, stirring occasionally. Turn into deep dish, and garnish with slices of egg.

Lobster Patés.

Make puff paste and spread on very deep paté pans. Bake it empty. Having boiled well two or three fine lobsters, extract all the meat and mince very small, mixing it with coral smoothly mashed and yolk of hard-boiled egg, grated. Season with a little salt, cayenne, and powdered mace or nutmeg, adding a little yellow lemon rind, grated. Moisten mixture well with cream, fresh butter, or salad oil. Put it into stewpan, add very little water, let stew till it just comes to a boil. Take off the fire, and the patés being baked, remove them from tin pans, place them on large dish, and fill them up to the top with the mixture. Similar patés may be made of prawns or crabs.

Clam Fritters.

Fifty small or twenty-five large clams; dry them in napkin. If large, cut them in two; put pint of flour into basin, add two well-beaten eggs, one-half pint milk, and nearly as much of clam liquor; beat batter till free from lumps, then stir in clams. Put lard or beef drippings into frying pan, heat it to boiling, then drop in clam batter by spoonful. Fry brown on one side, then turn and fry on the other.

To Boil Lobsters or Crabs.

The lobster is in good season from September to June, and should be purchased alive and plunged into boiling water in which a good proportion of salt has been mixed. Continue to boil, according to size, from twenty minutes to an hour. Crabs should be boiled in the same manner, but a little more than half the time is necessary.

POULTRY.

To Clean Poultry.

FIRST singe over blazing paper or alcohol, then cut off the feet and tips of the wings, and the neck as far as it looks dark. Then, with the blade of a knife, take out all the pin feathers. Now turn the skin of the neck back, and with the forefinger and thumb draw out the crop and wind-pipe; cut a slit in the lower part of the fowl, and draw out the intestines, being careful not to break the gall-bag, as it will spoil the flavor of the meat. It will be found near the upper part of the breast bone and attached to the liver. Now wash thoroughly in several waters and drain. If the poultry is at all strong, let it stand in water several hours with either charcoal or saleratus, after which rinse out well with clear water.

Roast Turkey.

Prepare as directed. Make a dressing of bread crumbs, and stuff, first the craw, and tie a string tightly about the neck to prevent the escape of the stuffing, and then the body of the turkey. Bake slowly four or five hours. Dredge with flour and baste often; at first with butter and water, afterward with the gravy in the dripping-pan. Roast to a fine brown, and if it threatens to darken too rapidly, lay a sheet of white paper over it until the lower part is also done. Stew the chopped giblets in just enough water to cover them, and when the turkey is lifted from the pan, add these, with the water in which they were boiled, to the drippings; thicken with browned flour, boil up once, and pour into the gravy boat. Serve with cranberry sauce.

Ragout of Turkey.

Cut the cold turkey from the bones, and into bits an inch long. Put into a saucepan the gravy left from the roast, with hot water to dilute it, should the quantity be small. Add a lump of butter the size of an egg, a teaspoonful of pungent sauce, a half teaspoonful of cloves, a large pinch of nutmeg, and a little salt. Let it boil, and put in the meat. Stew slowly for ten minutes, and stir in a tablespoonful of cranberry sauce, and a tablespoonful of browned flour wet with cold water. Boil up once, and serve in a covered dish.

Fricasseed Chicken.

Joint the chicken, and put them in a kettle with enough cold water to cover them. Boil slowly until tender, season with pepper, salt, and a piece of butter; have ready soda biscuits, split them open and butter them; thicken the broth with flour, lay the chicken on platter with biscuit, and pour over the gravy.

Smothered Chicken.

Rub the inside of the chicken with fine salt and a little pepper; sprinkle flour over the outside, put it, with a bit of butter, size of a butternut, and about a pint of water, in the dripping-pan; cover closely, and set in the oven, and cook one and one-half hours; baste frequently, turn once or twice so as to cook evenly, then remove the cover, and brown lightly. Add one-half cup of cream and a teaspoonful of flour to the gravy in the pan, boil up and serve.

Chicken Patés.

Chop meat of cold chicken fine, and season well. Make large cupful rich drawn butter, and, while on fire, stir in two eggs, boiled hard, minced very fine, also a little chopped parsley, then chicken meat. Let almost boil. Have ready some paté-pans of good paste, baked quickly to light brown. Slip from pans while hot, fill with mixture, and set in oven to heat. Arrange upon dish and serve hot.

Chicken Pie.

Take two full-grown chickens, or more if small, disjoint them, cut backbone, etc., small as convenient. Boil them with few slices of salt pork in water enough to cover them; let boil quite tender, then take out breast bone. After they boil, and scum is taken off, put in a little onion cut very fine —not enough to taste distinctly, just enough to flavor a little; rub some parsley very fine when dry, or cut fine when green— this gives pleasant flavor. Season well with pepper and salt, and few ounces good, fresh butter. When all is cooked well, have liquid enough to cover chicken, then beat two eggs, and stir in some sweet cream. Line five-quart pan with crust made like soda biscuit, only more shortening, put in chicken and liquid, cover with crust same as lining. Bake till crust is done.

Boned Chicken.

Boil a chicken in as little water as possible until meat will fall from bones; remove all skin, chop together light and dark parts; season with pepper and salt. Boil down liquid in which chicken was boiled, then pour it on meat; place in tin, wrap tightly in cloth, press with heavy weight several hours. When served, cut in thin slices.

Chicken Croquettes.

One pint of rich milk; let it come to a boil; thicken with two tablespoonfuls of butter and four of flour. Season with salt and pepper. The same should be very thick; add a beaten egg just as it is taken from the fire, one-half pound of chicken minced very fine, and seasoned with a little salt, one teaspoonful chopped parsley, one teaspoonful of lemon juice, and one teaspoonful chopped celery. Stir into the hot sauce, mix thoroughly, and spread on a platter until perfectly cold. Shape croquettes, roll in the beaten white of an egg and cracker dust, and fry to a nice brown.

Roast Goose.

Wash out and wipe dry the body of the goose, and to the usual dressing of bread crumbs, etc., add a tablespoonful of minced onion, half as much powdered sage, and some bits of salt pork. Put into the dripping-pan with two cupfuls of boiling water, and roast from two to three hours, basting often and very copiously. When half done, cover the breast with a stiff paste of flour and water, removing when you are ready to brown it. Take the fat from the gravy and thicken with browned flour. Serve with apple sauce.

Roast Duck.

Clean, wash, and wipe very carefully. To the usual dressing add a little sage and a minced shallot. Stuff and sew up as usual, reserving the giblets for the gravy. If they are tender they will roast in an hour and a half. Baste well, skim the gravy before putting in the giblets and thickening. The giblets should be stewed in a very little water, then chopped fine and added to the gravy in the dripping-pan with a chopped shallot and a spoonful of browned flour. Accompany with currant or grape jelly.

To use up Cold Duck.

Cut the meat from the bones and lay it in a saucepan with a little minced cold ham; pour on just enough water to cover it, and stir in a tablespoonful of butter. Cover and heat gradually until it is near boiling. Then add the gravy diluted with a little hot water, a great spoonful of catsup, one of Worcestershire sauce and one of currant jelly, and a tablespoonful of browned flour. Boil up once and serve.

Stewed Pigeons.

Clean and wash the pigeons thoroughly, and put in a pot with a cupful of water, to keep them from burning, and a tablespoonful of butter for each one. Shut the lid down tightly and cook *slowly* until they are a nice brown. Once in a while turn them, and see that each is well wet with the liquor. Take them out and cover in a warm place—a cullender set over a pot of hot water is best—while you make the gravy. Chop the giblets of the pigeon *very* small, with a little onion and parsley. Put into the gravy with pepper and salt, boil up, and thicken with browned flour. Return the pigeons to the pot, cover again tightly, and cook slowly until tender. If there should not be liquor enough in the pot to make the gravy, add boiling water before the giblets go in.

Broiled Squabs.

Wash them (when they are cleaned) and dry carefully with a cloth; then split down the back and broil. Season with pepper and salt, and butter liberally in dishing them.

Roast Squabs.

Lay them in rows in the oven, with a little water in the pan. Baste often with butter and water until they are half done, then with their own gravy. Thicken the gravy and boil up once; then pour into a gravy boat. The pigeons should lie close together on the dish.

MEATS.

*" Nearer as they came, a genial savour
Of certain stews and roast meats and pilaus-
Things which in hungry mortal's eyes find favour."*

Roast Beef.

The best pieces for roasting are the porterhouse and rib pieces. Have your butcher remove the bone and skewer the meat into shape. Dredge with flour, salt, and pepper, and roast in a quick oven. Baste frequently, at first with salt and water, afterward with the drippings. If you like your meat rare, allow about a quarter of an hour to a pound.

Boiled ham and corned beef should be left to cool in the water in which they are boiled.

Roast Beef with Yorkshire Pudding.

Set a piece of beef to roast on a grating or several sticks laid across a dripping-pan. Three-quarters of an hour before it is done mix the pudding and pour into the pan. Continue to roast the beef, letting the drippings fall on the pudding below.

When done cut the pudding in squares and lay around the meat, or separately, if preferred. Pour off fat in the dripping-pan before putting in the pudding.

Receipt for Pudding.

One pint of milk; one teaspoonful of salt; two cups of flour sifted with one heaping teaspoonful of Dr. Price's cream baking powder; four eggs beaten thoroughly; mix all together quickly, eggs, milk, and salt, then flour.

Stewed Beef and Mushrooms.

Take five pounds of beef (with as much tenderloin as possible), put in a pan, and set in the oven fifteen minutes; then take the meat and put it in a small porcelain kettle, and dredge with salt, pepper, a teaspoonful of mace, half of cloves, the same of allspice, and two spoonfuls of flour; now put in cold water enough to cover the meat and stew slowly, keeping the steam in, three hours. Then put in half a tumbler of mushroom catsup, and simmer half an hour longer. Serve with plenty of gravy.

Cannelon of Beef.

Chop the remains of cold roast beef, mix with a quarter of a pound of minced ham, season with pepper, salt, grated lemon-peel, and a little onion. Moisten with some of the gravy and bind with a beaten egg or two. Make some pie-paste, or such as you would use for dumplings, roll into an oblong sheet, put the minced meat in the middle, and make the pastry into a long roll, enclosing the meat. Close at the ends with round caps of pastry, the edges pinched well together. Lay in a dripping-pan, the joined side of the roll downward, and bake to a good brown.

Beefsteak.

Wipe the steak dry and broil upon a buttered gridiron, turning frequently whenever it begins to drip. When done, which should be in from twelve to fifteen minutes if the fire is clear and strong, lay upon a hot dish; season with pepper, salt and butter. Put over it a hot cover, and wait five minutes before sending to the table, to draw the juice to the surface and allow the seasoning to penetrate the steak.

Smothered Beef and Onions.

Take a good-sized steak (round is the best) and six onions; remove bone from steak; chop onions fine; pepper and salt·

place on steak and roll; fasten firmly, and put in a frying-pan, with a little water; cover closely, and steam about fifteen minutes. Then put a good-sized piece of butter in the pan, and cover again; steam till done, having just enough water in the pan to keep it from burning.

Pressed Corned Beef.

Cook the meat until the bones and gristle can be removed. Place in an earthen dish, with enough of the liquor to cover the meat when placed under a weight.

Savory Kidney Stew.

One beef kidney, cut into small pieces; put on in cold water, after removing *all* the fat; skim as it boils until all the scum is removed; then add two bay leaves, four whole cloves, four pepper-corns, salt and pepper to taste, two tablespoonfuls of vinegar, two good-sized potatoes cut into small pieces, one-half of an onion; boil until potatoes are soft and kidney tender; piece of butter the size of an egg, browned; a tablespoonful of flour, mixed in milk; stir flour into melted butter; then add this to stew; stir well and boil a few minutes. When ready to serve, add the juice of one-half lemon.

Beef's Heart.

Choose a fine fresh one; wash well; lay in salt and water an hour; then wipe dry; stuff with a force-meat of bread-crumbs, minced salt pork, pepper, salt, and chopped parsley, with a little onion; pack this in tightly; sew the heart up in a coarse net, fitted well to it, and stew one hour and a half in weak broth. (A cupful can be taken from your soup stock.) At the end of this time take it out, undo the cloth, and return the heart to the saucepan, with enough gravy to half-cover it;

add to this a tablespoonful of butter, cut up, in as much flour; pepper and salt to taste; cover closely, and simmer half an hour, turning as it browns; dish it; add the juice of half a lemon to the gravy, boil once, and pour over the heart.

Roast Mutton.

Wash the meat well, and dry with a cloth; let your fire be clear and strong: put the meat on, with a very little water, in the dripping-pan, and allow in roasting about twenty minutes to the pound; baste often, and if in danger of browning too fast, cover with a large sheet of white paper. Serve with currant jelly.

Boiled Mutton.

The best part for boiling is the leg. Put on in boiling water and cook, allowing about twenty minutes to the pound. Make a sauce by taking out a cupful of liquor when it is nearly done, cooling it until you can take off the fat, then heating again in a saucepan, and stirring into it one tablespoonful of butter, two teaspoonfuls of flour; wet up with cold water; stir five minutes, putting in a teaspoonful of chopped parsley; and, after another boil, take from the fire and add the juice of a lemon. When the liquor in which the meat is boiled is to be used for soup, salt slightly while cooking, sprinkling all over lightly with salt as soon as you take from the fire.

Mutton Chops and Tomato Purée.

Broil the chops, after trimming them neatly; rub, as soon as they leave the gridiron, with butter on both sides, pepper and salt, and cover for a few minutes in a hot dish. Make the purée by stewing a can of tomatoes until nearly dry, then seasoning and stirring in a tablespoonful of butter, rolled in flour; simmer three minutes. Arrange the chops on their sides, overlapping each other, inside of the curve of a flat dish, and pour the purée within their enclosure.

Roast Lamb.

Lay in the dripping-pan, dash a small cupful of boiling water over it, and roast in a quick oven, allowing about fifteen minutes to a pound; baste often and freely, and after half an hour, cover with a sheet of thick paper. Five minutes before taking it up remove this, dredge with flour, and, as this browns, bring to a froth with butter. Serve with mint sauce.

Lamb Chops.

Broil quickly over a clear fire; pepper and salt; butter on both sides.

Stewed Lamb with Mushroom Sauce.

Let your butcher take out the bones from the lower side of a shoulder of lamb, leaving in the shank. Fill the cavity thus left with a good force-meat of crumbs, chopped pork and sweet herbs, and sew the edges of meat together to hold it in. If you have no gravy ready, make about a pint of the lamb trimmings, it need not be strong. Put the lamb into a pot with some thin slices of salt pork laid in the bottom; pour in the gravy, cover tightly, and stew gently one hour. Then turn the meat and cook twenty minutes longer. Lay the lamb on a hot dish, and butter it all over. Cover and keep warm over hot water while you make the sauce. Have ready half a can of mushrooms boiled and chopped. Strain the gravy left in the pot, add the mushrooms, and stew five minutes; thicken with brown flour, boil up and pour over the lamb.

Roast Veal.

Wash the veal and rub in a good handful of salt. Make a dressing in the following manner and stuff it. Soak about two quarts of stale bread in cold water, chop fine a half pound of fat pork, mix this with the bread, and one teaspoonful of pepper, one of salt, one of sweet marjoram, one half teaspoonful of sage, and one egg or two crackers. Take out all the bones possible, and cut slits to make cavities for the dressing, then stuff and skewer securely. Cover the veal with thin slices of salt pork, heat gradually, baste frequently—at first with salt and water, afterward with the gravy. A piece of veal weighing eight pounds should cook, at least, three hours.

Veal Loaf.

Three and one-half pounds of the leg, fat and lean, a small slice of salt pork, both chopped fine, six small crackers pounded, two eggs, butter size of an egg, one tablespoon each of pepper, salt, and nutmeg; work all together in shape of a loaf, grate bread over the top, and also place bits of butter over it. Bake two hours in a dripping pan with a little water, basting often. Serve cold in slices.

Veal Pot Pie.

Take three pounds of veal, put in hot water enough to cover, cook slowly about three hours, or till tender; renew water as it boils away. Cook potatoes, either by themselves or with the meat, half an hour. Put meat, potatoes, and dumplings on platter and pour over gravy. Season with butter, pepper, and salt.

Dumplings.

One pint of flour, two rounded teaspoonfuls Dr. Price's cream baking powder, salt, sweet milk for a stiff batter. Drop by spoonfuls into boiling soup fifteen minutes before serving. Do not raise the cover or let the soup cease to boil after they are added.

Veal Scallop.

Chop some cold roast or stewed veal very fine, put a layer in the bottom of a buttered pudding dish, and season with pepper and salt. Next have a layer of finely powdered crackers. Strew some bits of butter upon it and wet with a little milk; then more veal seasoned as before, and another round of cracker crumbs, with butter and milk. When the dish is full wet well with gravy or broth, diluted with warm water. Spread over all a layer of cracker, seasoned with salt, wet into a paste with milk and bound with a beaten egg or two if the dish be large. Stick butter bits thickly over it: invert a tin pan so as to cover all and keep in the steam, and bake—if small, half an hour; three-quarters will suffice for a large dish. Remove the cover ten minutes before it is served, and brown.

Cannelon of Veal.

Two pounds of cold roast or stewed veal. The remains of a stewed and stuffed fillet are good for this purpose, especially if underdone. One pound cold boiled ham. One large cupfull gravy. If you have none left over, make it of the refuse bits of the cold meat, such as fat, skin, etc. One small teaspoonful finely minced lemon peel, the same of mace, and a tablespoonful chopped parsley, salt and pepper. One teacupful bread crumbs, dry and fine. Yolks of three eggs beaten light, reserving the whites for glazing the cannelon when done. Chop the meat very well, season it and stir in the beaten yolks; wet with half the gravy, and mix in the bread crumbs. It should be just soft enough to handle without running into a shapeless mass. Flour your hands, and make it into a roll about three times as long as it is broad. Flour the outside well and lay in a greased baking pan. Cover and set in the oven until it is smoking hot, when remove the cover and brown quickly. Draw to the oven-door and brush over with white of egg, shut the door for one minute to set this, and transfer the cannelon, by the help of a cake-turner or a wooden paddle, to a hot dish. Lay three-cornered pieces of fried bread close about it, and pour a rich gravy over all. You can make a really elegant dish of this by adding to the gravy a half-pint of sliced mushrooms, and stewing them in it until they are tender and savory, then pouring them over the *rouleau* of meat.

Veal Cutlets.

Two pounds veal cutlet nicely trimmed. One small onion, sliced. Four tablespoonfuls strained tomato sauce. Enough butter or clear dripping to fry the cutlets. Salt and pepper, with a bunch of sweet herbs. Half a cup gravy. Fry the cutlets to a light brown, but not crisp; take them out and put into a covered saucepan. Have ready the gravy in another, with the tomato sauce stirred into it. Fry the onion in the fat from which you have taken the cutlets and add with the fat to the gravy. Pour all over the cutlets and simmer, covered, twenty minutes.

Veal Croquettes.

Mince veal fine ; mix one-half cup of milk with one teaspoonful of flour, a piece of butter the size of an egg; cook until it thickens; stir into the meat; roll into balls; dip in egg, with a little milk stirred in ; roll in browned bread crumbs; fry in hot lard.

Brown Fricassee of Sweetbreads.

Four sweetbreads, two cups brown veal gravy, strong and well seasoned, four tablespoonfuls of butter, pinch of mace, and twice as much cloves, browned flour for thickening, one teaspoonful chopped onion, stewed in and then strained out of the gravy. Wash the sweetbreads carefully in warm water, removing every bit of skin and gristle. Lay them in a saucepan and cover with boiling water. Boil them ten minutes hard, turn off the hot water, and plunge them instantly into very cold, in which you have dissolved a little salt. Leave them in this about fifteen minutes, or until they are cool, white, and firm; cut each crosswise into slices nearly half an inch thick, have ready the butter in the frying pan, and fry the slices, turning frequently, until they are a good brown—but do not dry them up. Drain off the fat through a cullender, lay the sliced sweetbreads within a saucepan, pour the hot brown gravy, already seasoned, over them, cover closely, and simmer, not boil, fifteen minutes longer.

Sweetbreads.

Scald in salted water; remove stringy parts; put in cold water five or ten minutes; drain in towel; dip in egg and bread or cracker crumbs, fry in butter, or boil them plain.

Roast Leg of Pork.

One weighing about seven pounds is enough—even for a large family. Score the skin in parallel lines running from side to side; put it down to roast with a *very* little water in the pan; heat gradually, until the fat begins ooze from the meat, when quicken the fire; baste only with its own gravy, and do this often, that the skin may not be hard and tough.

When done take it up, skim the gravy thoroughly, add a little boiling water, thicken with brown flour, add pepper, salt, and the juice of half a lemon. Serve with apple sauce.

Roast Spare Rib.

When first put down to the fire cover with a greased paper, until it is half done; remove it then and dredge with flour. A few minutes later, baste once with butter and afterward with its own gravy. This is necessary, the spare-rib being a very dry piece. Just before you take it up strew over the surface fine bread crumbs, seasoned with powdered sage, pepper, and salt. Let it cook from five to ten minutes and baste once more with butter; skim the gravy, add a half cupful of hot water, and thicken with brown flour.

Boiled Ham.

Soak in cold water over night. Next morning wash hard with a coarse cloth or brush, and put on to boil with plenty of cold water. Allow a quarter of an hour to each pound in cooking, and do not boil too fast. Do not remove the skin until cold; it will come off easily then, and the juices are better preserved than when it is stripped hot.

Ham and Eggs.

Cut your slices of ham of a uniform size and shape; fry quickly, and take them out of the pan as soon as they are done. Have the eggs, and drop them, one at a time, in the hissing fat; have a large pan for the purpose, that they may not run together. In three minutes they will be done. The meat should be kept hot, and when the eggs are ready lay one on each slice of ham, which should have been cut the proper size for this.

GAME.

Haunch of Venison.

Wash thoroughly with luke warm water and vinegar; then rub well with butter or lard to soften the skin; cover it on the top and sides with a thick paste of flour and water nearly half an inch thick. Lay upon this a large sheet of thin white wrapping paper, well buttered, and above this thick foolscap. Keep all in place by greased pack thread; then put down to roast with a little water in the dripping pan. Let the fire be steady and strong. Pour a few tablespoonsful of butter and water over the meat now and then, to keep the paper from scorching. If the haunch is large, it will take at least five hours to roast. About half an hour before you take it up, remove the paper and paste, and test with a skewer in the thickest part. If it goes in readily close the oven and let it brown for half an hour. Baste three or four times with butter and water; at last dredge with flour, and rub over with butter to make a froth. Take up and put on a hot dish. Skim the gravy left in the pan, strain and thicken with browned flour; add two teaspoonfuls of currant jelly, and pepper and salt. Boil up for an instant and pour into a gravy-boat. *Always* serve currant jelly with venison.

Fricasseed Rabbit.

Clean two young rabbits, and cut into joints, and soak in salt and water one hour. Put into a sauce-pan with a pint of cold water, a bunch of sweet herbs, an onion finely chopped, a pinch of mace, one of nutmeg, pepper, and a half pound of salt pork cut into strips. Cover and stew until tender. Take out the rabbits and place in a dish where they will keep warm. Add to the gravy a cup of rich milk, two well beaten-eggs stirred in a little at a time, and a tablespoonful of butter. Boil up once, when you have thickened with flour wet in cold milk, and take the saucepan from the fire. Squeeze in the juice of a lemon stirring all the while, and pour over the rabbits. Do not cook the head or neck.

Grouse Roasted with Bacon.

Clean, trim and stuff as usual. Cover the entire bird with bacon binding all with buttered pack-thread. Roast three-quarters of an hour, basting with butter and water three times, then with the dripping. When quite done, dish with the bacon laid about the bird. Skim the gravy, thicken with browned flour, season with pepper and the juice of a lemon, and boil up once.

Quails are roasted in the same way.

Wild Pigeon (Stewed).

Clean and wash very carefully, then lay in salt water for an hour. Rinse the inside with soda water, shaking it about well; wash out with clear water, and stuff with force-meat made of bread-crumbs and chopped salt pork, seasoned with pepper. Sew up the pigeons and put on to stew in enough cold water to cover them, and allow to each a fair slice of fat bacon cut into narrow strips. Season with pepper and a pinch of nutmeg; take from the gravy and lay in a covered dish to keep warm. Strain the gravy, add the juice of a lemon and a tablespoonful of currant jelly, thickened with browned flour. Boil up and pour over the pigeons.

Partridge.

In dressing partridges, skin instead of picking them. Put in water with two sage leaves and a little onion. When cooked done, add cream, butter, pepper and salt, and thicken the gravy with a little corn starch.

SAUCES FOR MEAT AND FISH.

"Hunger is the best sauce."

Bread Sauce.

Quarter and boil one large onion with some black peppers and milk, till onion is quite a pulp. Pour milk strained on grated white stale bread, and cover it. In an hour put it into a saucepan, with a good piece of butter mixed with a little flour; boil the whole up together and serve.

Bread Sauce for Partridges or Grouse.

One cup of stale bread crumbs, one onion, two ounces butter, pepper and salt, a little mace. Cut the onion fine and boil it in milk till quite soft; then strain the milk on to the stale bread crumbs and let it stand an hour. Put it in a saucepan with the boiled onion, pepper, salt and mace. Give it a boil, and serve in sauce tureen. This sauce can also be used for grouse, and is very nice. Roast partridges are nice served with bread crumbs, fried brown in butter, with cranberry or currant jelly laid beside them in the platter.

Caper Sauce.

Two tablespoonfuls butter, one tablespoonful flour; mix well; pour on boiling water till it thickens; add one hard-boiled egg chopped fine, and two tablespoonfuls capers.

Drawn Butter.

One half cup butter, two tablespoonfuls flour, rubbed thoroughly together, then stir into pint boiling water; little salt; parsley if wished.

Gravy for Roast Meats.

After taking out meat, pour off fat; add water, season and thicken with flour.

Gravy for Turkey.

Boil giblets very tender; chop fine; then take liquor in which they are boiled, thicken with flour; season with salt, pepper, and a little butter; add giblets and dripping in which turkey was roasted.

Horse-radish Sauce.

One dessertspoonful of olive oil, same quantity of powdered mustard, one tablespoonful of vinegar, one of grated horseradish and one teaspoonful of salt.

Oysters Sauce.

One pint of oysters, two tablespoonfuls of butter rolled well in flour, one cup of milk. Heat the oyster liquor and when it boils skim and put in the oysters. When they boil stir in the butter and flour. Boil five minutes and put with the milk which has been heated in another vessel. Stir up well and pour out.

Sauce for Boiled Cod and other kinds of Fish.

To one gill boiling water add as much milk; stir into this while boiling two tablespoonfuls butter gradually, one tablespoonful flour wet up with cold water; as it thickens, the chopped yolk one boiled egg and one raw egg beaten light. Take directly from fire, season with pepper, salt, a little chopped parsley and juice one lemon, and set covered in boiling water (but not over fire) five minutes, stirring occasionally. Pour part of sauce over fish when dished; the rest in a boat. Serve mashed potatoes with it.

Sauce for Salmon and other Fish.

One cupful milk heated to a boil and thickened with tablespoonful corn starch previously wet up with cold water, the liquor from the salmon, one gravyspoonful butter, one raw egg beaten light, juice one-half lemon, mace, and cayenne pepper to taste. Add the egg to thickened milk when you have stirred in butter and liquor; take from fire, season and let stand in hot water three minutes, covered. Lastly put in lemon juice and turn out immediately. Pour it all over and around the salmon.

Tomato Sauce.

Pare, slice and stew tomatoes for twenty minutes, strain and rub through a sieve, leaving hard and tough parts behind. Put into a saucepan with a little minced onion, parsley, pepper, salt and sugar. Bring to boil; stir in good spoonful butter rolled in flour. Boil up and serve.

Mint Sauce.

Mix one tablespoonful white sugar to one-half teacupful good vinegar; add mint chopped fine; one-half teaspoonful salt. Serve with roast lamb or mutton.

Cranberry Jelly.

Take one quart cranberries, put in kettle, add one cup water, let come to a boil and then add two cups sugar; let boil ten minutes and then strain in moulds for use.

Apple Sauce.

Pare, core, and slice tart apples, and stew in water enough to cover them until they break to pieces. Beat to a pulp with a good lump of butter and plenty of sugar. Eat cold.

Dressing for Fowls.

One quart bread crumbs which have been chopped, not soaked; add one slice of salt pork, chopped to a cream; season with salt, pepper, sage, and a generous supply of butter; beat in one or two eggs. The best authorities say that dressing is the finest when it crumbles as the fowl is cut.

Oyster Dressing.

One quart oysters, add bread crumbs till you can mould like a loaf of bread, butter size of two eggs, pepper, salt and sage to taste.

EGGS.

"O, egg! within thine oval shell,
What palate-tickling joys do dwell."

Boiled Eggs.

Put them on in cold water, and let them come to a boil which will be in about ten minutes. The inside white and yolk will then be of the consistency of custard.

Poached Eggs.

Strain some water into a frying-pan, which must be also perfectly clean. When the water boils break the eggs separately into a saucer. Take the pan off and slip the eggs one by one carefully upon the surface. When all are in put back on the fire and boil gently three minutes. Take out with a perforated skimmer, drain and lay upon slices of toasted bread, well buttered, and in a hot dish. Add pepper and salt, and garnish with parsley.

Baked Eggs.

Have a good piece of butter in the frying pan, and when it is hot, drop in the eggs, taking care that each is whole. Sprinkle with pepper and salt. Put into the oven and bake until the whites are well set. Serve very hot, with buttered toast.

Scrambled Eggs.

Put a good piece of butter in a frying-pan, and when it is hot drop in the eggs, which should be broken whole into a bowl.

Stir in with them a little chopped parsley, some pepper and salt, and keep stirring to and fro, up and down, for three minutes. Turn out at once into a hot dish and eat without delay.

Creamed Eggs.

Boil six eggs twenty minutes. Make one pint of cream sauce. Have six slices of toast on a hot dish. Put a layer of sauce on each slice of toast, then the whites of the eggs cut in strips; and over this the yolks rubbed through a sieve. Place in the oven for about three minutes. Garnish with parsley and serve.

Scalloped Eggs.

Make a force-meat of chopped or ground ham, fine bread crumbs, pepper, salt and some melted butter. Moisten with milk to a soft paste, and half fill some paté pans with the mixture. Break an egg carefully upon the top of each, dust with pepper and salt, and sift some finely powdered cracker over all. Set in the oven and bake until the eggs are well set—about eight minutes. Eat hot.

Egg Basket.

Make these for breakfast the day after you have had roast chicken, duck, or turkey for dinner. Boil six eggs hard. Cut neatly in half and extract the yolks. Rub these to a paste with some melted butter, pepper and salt and set aside. Pound the minced meat of the cold fowl fine in the same manner and mix with the egg paste, moistening with melted butter as you proceed, or with a little gravy if you have it to spare. Cut off a slice from the bottoms of the hollowed whites of the egg, to make them stand, fill with the paste, arrange close together on a flat dish, and pour over them the gravy left from yesterday's roast, heated boiling hot, and mellowed by a few spoonfuls of cream or rich milk.

Omelet.

Five eggs, beaten separately, the whites to a stiff froth that will stand alone, the yolks to a smooth, thick batter. Add to the yolks five tablespoonfuls of milk, pepper and salt, lastly stir in the whites lightly. Have ready in a hot frying pan, a good lump of butter. When it hisses, pour in your mixture gently and cook carefully on top of the stove for about ten minutes. When well set put in the oven to brown—fold it and serve hot.

5

SALADS.

The Spanish proverb says that, "to make a perfect salad, there should be a miser for oil, a spendthrift for vinegar, a wise man for salt, and a madcap to stir the ingredients up and mix them well together."

Salad Dressing.

The yolks of six eggs beaten strongly; add three tablespoonfuls of dry mustard, and mix; one teaspoonful salt (celery salt if you like it), a pinch of cayenne pepper, one-half pint of Price's Imperial olive oil, or half oil and half butter, two-thirds of a pint of vinegar. Mix all these thoroughly, and put dish in boiling water, and stir until it is as thick as thick cream. This makes nearly a quart of dressing, and will keep a long time.

Lobster Salad.

Boil two live lobsters about thirty minutes. Break the shells and take out the solid meat, cut into cubes, place in a deep dish, and season with salt, pepper, Price's Imperial olive oil, and vinegar. Have the hearts from four heads of lettuce in the salad bowl; turn in the lobster, and cover with mayonnaise dressing. Garnish the dish with pitted olives and hard-boiled eggs.

Lobster Salad Without Oil.

One fine lobster boiled thoroughly, and carefully picked out. Cut into small pieces, put in a broad dish, and sprinkle with a teaspoonful of salt and pepper. Set aside in a cold place. Dressing—two large tablespoonfuls of butter, one and one-half tablespoonfuls of flour or corn starch, one pint of boiling water. Stir the flour, previously wet, into the boiling water; let it boil two minutes, and add butter. Boil one minute longer and set aside to cool. In the meantime, mix well and smoothly one large tablespoonful of mustard, one teaspoonful of powdered sugar, one-half teaspoonful of salt, one tablespoonful of boiling water, and one small cup of vinegar. Beat this up well, then add to the drawn butter, beat to a cream and pour over the lobster. Garnish with celery tops and hard-boiled eggs.

Chicken Salad.

Take equal parts of cold boiled chicken (or turkey) and celery. Mince the meat well. Remove every scrap of fat, gristle, and skin; cut the celery into bits half an inch long, mix well together and pour over mayonnaise dressing.

Mayonnaise Dressing.

Yolks of four hard-boiled eggs; one teacup of Price's Imperial olive oil, rubbed in after the eggs are powdered, yolks of two raw eggs mixed in, one teaspoonful of French mustard dissolved in vinegar, cayenne pepper, and salt; put them in chicken and dressing. Juice of one lemon. This amount is for one chicken.

Potato Salad.

Cut six large cold potatoes in squares, put in a dish and season as follows : two tablespoonfuls of Price's Imperial olive oil, one-half teaspoonful mustard, pepper, salt, and celery salt; whip to smooth paste and add slowly five teaspoonfuls

SALADS.

of vinegar; when mixed pour on the salad, and serve. A little chopped onion can be mixed in if desired, and also young lettuce leaves, cut fine.

Boiled Dressing for Cabbage Salad.

One-half cup of vinegar and two tablespoonfuls sugar boiled together; add one-half saltspoonful of pepper, one-half teaspoonful of salt, one-half teaspoonful of dry mustard, one tablespoonful of butter and one tablespoonful of flour creamed together. Mix all together until smooth, and pour over the beaten yolk of one egg. Pour this over thinly shaved cabbage while hot.

VEGETABLES.

" The onion strong, the parsnip sweet,
The twining bean, the ruddy beet ;
Yea, all the garden brings to light
Speak it a landscape of delight."

HAVE them as fresh as possible. Stale and withered ones are unwholesome. Pick over and wash thoroughly in cold water. It is well to lay them in cold water for some time before cooking. Be sure they are thoroughly done, drain well, and *serve hot*.

Boiled Potatoes.

Boil in cold water with a pinch of salt. Cook steadily until a fork will pierce easily to the heart of the largest. Then pour off every drop of water, sprinkle with salt, and set back on the range, a little to one side, with the lid off. Let them dry a few minutes and serve in uncovered dish.

Mashed Potatoes.

Pare and let them lie in cold salted water for an hour or two. Boil until done, drain thoroughly, sprinkle with salt, and mash them in the pot with potato-beetle, working in a tablespoonful of butter and enough milk to make the paste about the consistency of soft dough. Form into a mound with wooden spoon, and leave dots of pepper on the surface.

Baked Chopped Potatoes.

For a three-quart pudding dish pare twenty-five medium-sized potatoes. Chop, not too fine, place in dish and stir in salt and pepper, and fill the dish up with milk. Bake one hour and a half in a hot oven.

Escalloped Potato.

Cover the bottom of a baking dish with a layer of sliced, cold boiled potatoes; cover with finely powdered cracker, adding pepper, salt, and pieces of butter; fill the dish with layers of potato and cracker; when full pour over the top layer a cupful of sweet cream and bake one hour.

Potato Puff.

Take two cupfuls of cold mashed potato, and stir into it two tablespoonfuls of melted butter, beating to a cream. Then add two eggs, beaten very light, and a teacupful of cream or milk, salting to taste. Beat all well, pour into a deep dish, and bake in a quick oven until nicely browned.

Potato Croquettes.

Season cold mashed potatoes with salt, pepper, and butter; moisten with sweet milk or cream; mix thoroughly with this one beaten egg, and make into small rolls, being careful to have the surface perfectly smooth. Fry a rich golden brown in hot lard.

Warmed-up Potatoes.

Put into a saucepan two tablespoonfuls of butter, a little parsley chopped small, salt and pepper to taste. Stir up well until hot, add a small cup of cream or rich milk, thicken with a teaspoonful of flour, and stir until it boils. Chop some cold boiled potatoes, put into the mixture, and boil up once before serving.

Sweet Potatoes.

Boil until they are nearly done, when peel and bake brown, basting with butter several times, but draining dry before they go to the table.

Lyonnaise Potatoes.

Put a piece of butter the size of an egg in frying-pan with one small, finely chopped onion. When this is browned put in slices of cold boiled potatoes; turn carefully until brown, add a teaspoonful of finely chopped parsley, salt and pepper.

Saratoga Fried Potatoes.

Wash the potatoes clean, pare and slice very thin, throw into cold water long enough to take out some of the starch, then wipe dry and put into boiling lard, a few pieces at a time. As soon as they are of a clear golden brown, skim out and drain in a cullender or sieve.

Salsify or Oyster Plant.

Scrape the roots, dropping into cold water as soon as possible; exposure to the air blackens them. Cut in pieces an inch long, put in a saucepan with hot water enough to cover them, and stew until tender. Turn off the water, and add a cupful of milk. Stew about ten minutes after this begins to boil, put in a great lump of butter, cut into bits and roll in flour; pepper and salt to taste.

Egg Plant.

Slice the egg plant half an inch thick; pare and lay in salt water for an hour or more. Wipe dry, dip in beaten egg, then in cracker crumbs, and fry in hot lard until well done and nicely browned.

Miss F.'s Egg Plant.

Select one that is firm and fresh. Peel it with a sharp knife, so that the smooth outline is not broken. If large, the plant is then cut into quarters; if medium in size, into halves. Let it lie for half an hour in salt water. Then put it into boiling water with a little salt. It is cooked enough when it can be easily pierced with a straw. While the egg plant is boiling, prepare the onion, which is to give its slight pungency to the egg plant. Cut one medium sized onion into very small pieces, and cover it with salt water. In ten minutes pour off the water, and put the chopped onion into a hot skillet with a little butter and fry it brown. It is absolutely essential that the onion should be thoroughly cooked and brown. Drain the egg plant in a cullender, and put it in a large earthenware bowl. With a silver fork stir it until it is broken up, but do not really mash it, or it will not be light when finished. Mix with the egg plant an amount equal in bulk to itself of rolled bread crumbs; then add the browned onion and one well beaten egg; season with salt, pepper, and a dessertspoonful of butter. Put this all into a well buttered earthen dish, and bake until nicely browned, but not until dried, as the ingredients, with the exception of the egg, were all cooked before being put into the oven. Serve hot in the dish in which it was baked. It is excellent if warmed again the next day.—*Good Housekeeping.*

Stewed Tomatoes.

Peel and cut them up, extracting the cores or hard part of the stem end, and stew half an hour. Add salt and pepper to taste, a teaspoonful of sugar, and a tablespoonful of butter. Stew gently fifteen minutes longer, and serve.

Escalloped Tomatoes.

Place in a baking dish a layer of bread crumbs, then a layer of peeled sliced tomatoes with bits of butter, a little salt and pepper, then bread crumbs, tomatoes, etc., until the dish is full, having the bread crumbs on top.

Asparagus.

Cut stalks of equal length, and tie in bundles; boil in salted water for twenty minutes, have ready slices of nicely toasted bread; dip these in the asparagus liquor, butter them, and lay on a hot dish; drain the asparagus, untie, and arrange on toast; pour over all hot cream, seasoned with butter, or drawn butter can be used instead of the cream.

Stewed Celery.

Wash and scrape the tender white part of two heads of celery, cut in pieces two inches long, cover with boiling water, and simmer gently half an hour. Drain, if necessary, and add rich milk or cream, thicken slightly with corn starch, season well with butter, pepper, and salt.

Parsnips.

Scrape off the skin, and cut in thick, lengthwise slices. Dredge with flour, and fry in hot lard or dripping, turning when one side is brown. Drain off every drop of fat, add salt and pepper, and serve hot.

String Beans.

Cut off each end, and remove strings. Put in boiling water, and cook at least two hours, or until tender. If necessary, drain; then add butter, pepper, and salt.

Pease.

Shell, and put in boiling water, and cook until tender. Drain, and season with salt, pepper, and butter. If liked, add a cup of sweet cream.

Succotash.

This is made of green corn and lima beans. Have a third more corn than beans, when the corn has been cut from the cobs, and the beans shelled. An hour and a half before dinner put the cobs and beans into cold water to boil; after one hour take out the cobs and put in the corn, and boil half an hour. Add butter, pepper, and salt, and serve.

Boston Baked Beans.

To one pint of dry beans allow a full half-pound of pork, a large spoonful each of molasses and salt, one teaspoonful each of sugar and mustard. Soak the beans over night; in the morning put them in fresh water, and cook slowly until tender, but do not let them break to pieces. Skim out of this water into a quart bean pot, mix molasses, sugar, etc., together in hot water enough to fill the pot; cut the rind of pork in squares, and put in with the beans. As the water cooks away, fill the pot with more, adding the last water within three hours of serving. Cook slowly from eight to ten hours or longer.

Baked Macaroni.

Break half a pound of pipe macaroni in pieces an inch long, and put in a saucepan of boiling water, slightly salted. Stew gently twenty minutes. It should be soft, but not broken or split. Drain well, and put a layer in the bottom of pudding dish; upon this grate some mild cheese and scatter over it bits of butter. Then more macaroni and cheese until the dish is full, having macaroni at the top; butter well, without the cheese. Add a small cup of cream or milk, and a very little salt. Bake, covered, half an hour; then brown nicely, and serve in the bake dish.

Baked Macaroni and Tomatoes.

Break half a pound of macaroni in pieces half an inch long, and boil about twenty minutes in boiling water, slightly salted. Stew from six to eight tomatoes till soft, add butter, pepper, and salt. Cover the bottom of a baking dish (well buttered) with a layer of macaroni, then tomatoes, until the dish is full, having the macaroni on top. Put pieces of butter over it, and bake in a quick oven about thirty minutes.

Rice Croquettes.

One cup of cold boiled rice, one teaspoonful of sugar and half as much salt, one teaspoonful melted butter, one egg beaten light, enough milk to make the rice into stiff paste. Sweet lard for frying. Work rice, butter, egg, etc., into an adhesive paste, beating each ingredient thoroughly into the mixture. Flour your hands and make the rice into oval balls. Dip each in beaten egg, then in flour or cracker dust, and fry in boiling lard, a few at a time, turning each with great care. When the croquettes are of a fine yellow brown, take out with a wire spoon, and lay within a heated cullender to drain off every drop of fat. Serve hot, with sprigs of parsley laid about them, in an uncovered dish.

Boiled Rice.

Pick over carefully, and wash in two waters, letting it stand in the last until you are ready to boil it. Have ready some boiling water, slightly salted, and put in the rice. Boil it twenty minutes, and do not put a spoon in it, but shake up hard and often, holding the cover on with the other hand. When done, drain off the water, and set the saucepan, uncovered, upon the range—where the rice will dry, not burn—five minutes. Eat with boiled mutton or fowls.

BREAD.

"Here is bread, which strengthens man's heart, and therefore is called the staff of life."

IN making bread during cold weather, the flour should be thoroughly warmed before mixing. Care should be taken to have the yeast fresh, and to keep the dough from getting chilled while rising.

To Cut Warm Bread.

Heat a thin-bladed knife on the stove or in boiling water.

Bread.

To four quarts of water put one Fleischmann & Co. compressed yeast cake; make a sponge and let it stand over night in a moderately warm place to rise. In the morning add one tablespoonful of salt; put in flour, and mix as soft as it can be handled. Knead the bread faithfully and from all sides until your hands will not adhere to the dough. Set the dough to rise where it will be kept in an even temperature. When light divide into as many loaves as you wish, and put into well-greased pans for the final rising. Set the pans in a warm place for an hour longer, with a cloth thrown over them. Then bake. The oven should not be too hot. This makes seven loaves.

Fine Bread.

Take a scant quart of water, as warm as milk from the cow; dissolve in it half a cake of Fleischmann's compressed yeast and a teaspoonful of salt. Have ready warmed two quarts of flour, full measure. Make a hole in the centre of the flour; see that the yeast is thoroughly dissolved in the water; pour it into the hole, working the flour gradually into it with the right hand. When mixed, this will be a soft dough. If too soft to work, sprinkle a little flour from a dredger and knead it, but always use as little as possible to knead with. At first, to a novice, it may seem sticky and unmanageable, but by degrees, always working from the sides toward the centre, the rough mass will become smooth and no longer sticky to the hands or bowl. When the dough is quite smooth and does not stick, let it rise. It will take perhaps two hours in a warm spot—eighty-five degrees to ninety degrees will be best. When it is quite light—that is, about double the bulk—work it over thoroughly. Set it to rise again before putting it in the pans, if you have time; if not, divide the dough into two and put it in well-buttered pans. Let it rise. It will take about an hour in mild weather, but never judge entirely by time; look to the bulk; if it is rather less than twice the size in an hour it is ready; if not, wait till it swells more. Some like a very light, porous bread; they may then let the loaf rise to more than double the bulk.

Graham Bread.

Make a sponge of one cup of warm water and one-half a cake of Fleischmann & Co.'s compressed yeast dissolved in it, thickened with flour. Let it rise over night, or until very light. Then add one-half cup of molasses, with one teaspoonful of soda dissolved in it, one teaspoonful of salt, one-half cup of milk, and graham flour enough to make a stiff batter; stir briskly, put in the oven at once, and bake slowly one hour and a half.

Parker House Rolls.

One pint milk, one tablespoonful lard (melted in the milk), two teaspoonfuls salt, three-quarters of a cake of Fleischmann's compressed yeast soaked in a cup of lukewarm water; make this into a soft sponge, and let it rise four hours; then roll it out about half an inch thick, and cut with a goblet; spread with melted butter and turn over not quite half. Put them in the pans, and let them rise for half an hour. Bake in a quick oven.

Parker House Rolls.

Scald one pint of sweet milk, and, when partly cooled, melt in it one-half cup white sugar and one tablespoonful of lard or butter. When lukewarm, add three-quarters of a cake of Fleischmann's compressed yeast, dissolved in one-half cup warm water, and place the mixture in centre of two quarts of flour. When light, knead thoroughly; let rise again; then knead again ten or fifteen minutes; then roll out thinner than for biscuit. Cut out, as for biscuit, and spread butter over half the surface, fold half over, and place in tins so as not to touch each other. Let rise again, and, when light, bake in quick oven.

Boston Brown Bread.

Two quarts of unbolted rye meal mixed with a quart of yellow corn meal; add a cup of molasses in which is dissolved a teaspoonful of salt and a large teaspoonful of soda; add cold water, working it with the hands into a very stiff loaf; put it into a buttered pan, smoothing over the top and wetting it; then steam it at least four hours, for the longer corn and rye meals are cooked the better; then set it for half an hour in a moderately quick oven to dry it off and produce a good crust. This is the genuine article, without which no Boston Sunday breakfast is complete.

Brown Bread.

Take two even cups of Hecker's Brown Bread Self-Raising Flour, one cup of cold water or milk, one-fourth to one-half a cup of molasses to suit the taste; mix thoroughly and pour it into a three-pint brown bread tin boiler that has been well greased, or a tin pail tightly covered will answer, set it into a steam cooker or covered iron kettle part full of boiling water, to steam four or five hours. Be careful not to allow any cessation in the boiling.

If the batter is allowed to steam eight or ten hours, the loaf becomes darker and richer. When done steaming, take the cover off the mould and put it, with the bread, into the oven about ten minutes. This dries the outside and forms a tender crust.

A handful of raisins mixed into the batter is a great improvement.

When taken out of the pail, let the loaf stand ten minutes in a warm oven; then dip a sharp knife into cold water and cut in slices. This loaf is excellent for breakfast if re-steamed thirty minutes, or cut in slices and warmed in an oven.

Raised Graham Rolls.

One cup of water, one tablespoonful of lard or butter, a little salt, one-half cake of Fleischmann's compressed yeast dissolved in one-half cup of warm water, half a cup flour; add graham flour to make a stiff batter. Let it rise over night and in the morning add one egg, three tablespoonfuls of molasses, half a teaspoonful of soda and one-third cup of Indian meal. Beat thoroughly, put in the gem-pans to rise, and bake in a quick oven.

Wheat Gems.

Mix one heaping teaspoonful of Dr. Price's cream baking powder in one pint of flour; add the yolks of two eggs, one tablespoonful of butter, one teacup of sweet milk, a pinch of salt. Mix well, beat the whites of the eggs to a stiff froth, stir in, and bake immediately in greased gem pans.

Graham Gems.

One and a half pints graham flour sifted dry, with three teaspoonfuls of Dr. Price's cream baking powder; rub in a tablespoonful of butter, salt, one beaten egg, half a cup of sugar, stir all with cool sweet milk to a batter, drop into gem pans or muffin rings and bake in a hot oven.

Pop Overs.

Two cups of sweet milk, two scant cups of flour, three eggs, salt. Beat eggs light; then add milk and flour and beat all five minutes. Pour into hot gem-irons and bake in a quick oven.

Muffins.

One pint of flour; one cup of milk; one egg; one tablespoonful of Dr. Price's cream baking powder; butter the size of a walnut.

Baking Powder Biscuit.

Put one quart of flour before sifting into a sieve, with three teaspoonfuls Dr. Price's cream baking powder, one of salt; mix all thoroughly with the flour, run through sieve, rub in two tablespoonfuls of butter, wet with half pint sweet milk; roll on board about an inch thick, cut with biscuit cutter, and bake in a quick oven fifteen minutes. If you have not milk use a little more butter and wet with water. Handle as little and make as rapidly as possible.

Corn Cake.

One cup of flour, one and one-half cups of meal, one egg, butter the size of an egg, one teaspoonful soda; one-fourth cup sugar, sour milk to make consistency of sponge cake; bake slowly.

Corn Cake.

Mix one cup each of flour and Indian meal, two heaping teaspoonfuls of Dr. Price's cream baking powder and a little salt together. Mix one egg, one-half cup sugar, butter size of an egg and one cup warm sweet milk together; then pour the liquid into the dry mixture; beat well and bake.

Waffles.

One quart of flour, two good teaspoonfuls of Dr. Price's cream baking powder, one-half cup butter, three eggs, and sufficient milk to make as thick as muffins. Add at the last about half cup of cold water. Cook in waffle irons over a hot fire.

Wheat Griddle Cakes.

One pint of sweet milk, two tablespoonfuls of butter, salt, two eggs beaten light, flour for a batter, with two teaspoonfuls of Dr. Price's cream baking powder. Beat all thoroughly; fry on a griddle greased with a piece of salt pork.

Buckwheat Griddle Cakes.

One quart of buckwheat flour, three large teaspoonfuls Dr. Price's cream baking powder, a little salt, mix to a batter with milk or water—water is best—and bake on a griddle well greased. As the batter is thin, more baking powder is required than for dough.

Buckwheat Cakes.

One quart lukewarm water; make a batter with the buckwheat flour; salt; three-quarters of a cake of Fleischmann's compressed yeast; dissolve in the warm water, and let rise over night; in the morning add a teaspoonful of soda and a little milk, which browns them.

Buckwheat Cakes.

To three pounds of Hecker's self-raising buckwheat add five pints of cold water or milk, or part each, and bake immediately. Keep the batter in a cool place if not wanted for immediate use. This will produce seventy light and delicious cakes, preferred by many to those made with yeast.

Oatmeal Porridge.

To one quart of boiling water add one cup of Hornby's steam cooked oats and one teaspoonful salt. Stir the oatmeal into the water while boiling and let it boil steadily, stirring up frequently from the bottom, for at least fifteen minutes. Send to the table in an uncovered dish, to be eaten with cream and sugar.

Boiled Mush.

One quart of boiling water, two cups of Indian meal, two tablespoons of flour, one teaspoonful of salt. Wet up meal and flour in a little cold water. Stir them in the water, which should be boiling hot when they go in. Boil at least half an hour, slowly, stirring deeply every few minutes, and constantly toward the last. Send to the table in a deep dish, but not covered, or the steam will render it clammy.

Hominy.

One quart of boiling water, two scant cups of Hecker's hominy, soaked over night in enough water to cover it well, and one teaspoonful of salt. Stir the hominy into the water while boiling, and let it boil steadily, stirring frequently for about half an hour. Send to table in uncovered dish.

Wheaten Grits.

In a pot of boiling water place a vessel fitted with a tight cover, containing a quart of milk or water, and when it is brought to the boiling point stir in slowly about five tablespoonfuls of Hecker's wheaten grits, and let it boil half an hour or one hour, stirring occasionally. By thus boiling it in a separate vessel, not in immediate contact with the fire, the risk of burning is obviated, without requiring constant stirring. Soaking the grits over night in the proper quantity of milk or water, and boiling as above, is considered a decided advantage.

WEIGHTS AND MEASURES.

ONE cup, medium size, holds—half a pint.
Two cups, medium size, of sifted flour weigh—half a pound.
One pint of sifted flour weighs—half a pound.
One pint of sugar weighs—one pound.
Two cupfuls of granulated sugar—one pound.
Two tablespoonfuls of liquid—one ounce.
Ten eggs—one pound.
One quart of flour—one pound.
One pint of finely chopped meat, packed solidly—one pound.
Butter, one pint—one pound when well packed.
A common-sized tumbler holds—half a pint.
One tablespoonful soft butter—one ounce.
One tablespoonful granulated suger—one ounce.
Four tablespoonfuls—half a gill.

CAKES.

"Wouldst thou both eat thy cake and have it?"

Hints for Making Cake.

FLOUR should always be sifted before using, and baking powder and cream tarter sifted with the flour. It is difficult to beat eggs light unless they are cold. Fresh lard is better to grease cake pans, than butter, and thin paper spread on the bottom of the pans, especially layer cake, helps them to turn out nicely. In mixing cake, first beat the butter to a cream, add the sugar, and then when beaten light, add the eggs, milk, flavoring, and spices; the flour last unless fruit is used, then save out a little flour from the measure to rub the fruit in.

White Cake.

Two cups of sugar, one-half cup of butter, one cup of milk, three cups of flour, the whites of four eggs, three teaspoonfuls of Dr. Price's baking powder. Beat the sugar and butter till light, then stir in the milk and flour, a little at a time, and add the whites of the eggs last.

Hickory Nut Cake.

Two cups of sugar, one-half cup of butter, three cups of flour, one cup of milk, whites of four eggs, three teaspoonfuls of Dr. Price's baking powder, two cups of chopped hickory nut meats.

Sponge Cake.

Ten eggs, their weight in sugar, half their weight in flour, the juice and rind of one lemon. Bake in a moderate oven one hour.

Angel's Cake.

Whites of eleven eggs, one and one-half goblets of pulverized sugar, one goblet of flour, one teaspoonful cream tartar in the flour, two teaspoonfuls of vanilla. Sift the flour and sugar separately six times, put the eggs, well beaten, on the sugar and stir, then put in the flour, a tablespoonful at a time; stir in two tablespoonfuls of hot water the last thing before putting it into the pan. Take a new pan with a tube in the centre, do not grease it. Bake forty minutes without opening the oven door. Let it cool in the pan turned bottom-side up over a sieve, or in a way that the heat will escape.

Cake Without Eggs.

Five cups of flour, two cups of sugar, one-half cup of butter, two cups of milk, one teaspoonful of soda, two of cream tartar, nutmeg and citron and raisins. This makes two loaves.

Fruit Cake.

One pound of butter, one pound of sugar, one pound of flour (reserving one-fourth of it to roll fruit in), ten eggs, one-half teaspoonful of soda, dissolved in a small spoonful of milk; three and one-half pounds of raisins, two pounds of currants and one-half pound of citron, four teaspoonfuls cinnamon, two teaspoonfuls cloves, one of grated nutmeg, one-half wineglass of rose water.

Minnehaha Cake.

One cup of sugar and a half-cup of butter, stirred to a cream. Whites of four eggs or five whole ones. Two teaspoonfuls of cream of tartar stirred into two heaping cups of sifted flour. One teaspoonful of soda in a half cup of milk. Bake in three layers. For filling between layers, a teacupful of sugar and a little water boiled till it is brittle when dropped in cold water; stir quickly the well-beaten white of an egg and a cup of stoned raisins chopped very fine. Place between and over the top.

Corn Starch Cake.

One cup of butter, two cups of sugar, two cups of flour, one cup of Duryea's corn starch, four eggs, one cup of milk, and two teaspoonfuls of Dr. Price's cream baking powder.

Gingerbread.

One egg, one-half cup of sugar, one-half cup of butter, one-half a cup of milk, two-thirds of a cup of molasses, two and one-half cups of flour, one teaspoonful of soda, and one of ginger.

Cookies.

Eight cups of flour, two cups of sugar, one cup of butter, one cup of sweet milk, one teaspoonful of vanilla, one heaping teaspoonful of Dr. Price's baking powder. Sprinkle white sugar over when rolled for cutting.

Doughnuts.

One cup of sugar, one cup of milk, two eggs, three teaspoonfuls of melted butter, nutmeg, and a little salt. One heaping teaspoonful of Dr. Price's baking powder. Flour to make soft dough. Cut out, and fry in hot fat.

Crullers.

One quart of flour, one and one-half cups of sugar, three tablespoonfuls of melted butter, three eggs, scant teacupful of sweet milk, two teaspoonfuls of Dr. Price's baking powder, a little nutmeg, and salt; make a soft dough, and fry in hot fat.

Ginger Wafers.

One-half cup each of butter, sugar, and molasses, one heaping teaspoonful of ginger, and a little salt. Let this come to a boil. Take from the fire and add immediately one teaspoonful of soda dissolved in a little water; while foaming, add flour to make very stiff. Roll very thin.

Hermit's.

One and one-half cups of sugar, one cup of butter, two eggs, one cup of currants or chopped raisins, one teaspoonful of soda in one-fourth of a cup of sweet milk, one teaspoonful of cloves, one of cinnamon, nutmeg, and allspice to taste. Put in flour as for cookies, roll thin, sprinkle with sugar before baking.

FILLING FOR LAYER CAKE.

Chocolate Caramel.

Two cups sugar, one-half cup sweet cream; boil together five minutes. Remove from the fire, flavor with vanilla, stir to a cream, and spread over the cake. Melt one-third of a cake of Fry's chocolate, and spread over the cream.

Sour Cream.

One cup of sour cream, one-half cup of sugar, one tablespoonful flour. Beat together and cook till it thickens, and when cold add one cup chopped walnuts.

Cream Custard.

Two eggs, three teaspoonfuls of Duryea's corn starch, half a cup of sugar, and one teaspoonful of vanilla. Scald a pint of milk, and stir the above in and boil two minutes.

Cocoanut.

One teacupful of cocoanut in enough rich milk to cook well, sweeten, and add the beaten whites of two eggs; the usual frosting for the top layer, with cocoanut sprinkled over it.

Raisin.

One cup of raisins, stoned and chopped fine and stirred into boiling frosting when cold.

Fig Filling.

One pound of figs chopped fine, stir in jelly or fruit juice till it will spread easily; add sugar, if necessary.

Lemon Filling.

One cup of sugar, one-fourth of a cup of butter, grated rind and juice of two lemons, yolks of four eggs, cook until it thickens, stirring all the while.

Jelly Cake.

Use Cairns' Scotch Home-made Jellies.

FROSTING.

Easy Frosting.

For one loaf of cake take the white of one egg, one full cup of powdered sugar and one teaspoonful of Duryea's corn starch. Beat the egg but little—not till light, then stir in the sugar and corn starch. When smooth spread it on your cake.

Boiled Frosting.

Take one pound of granulated sugar, put in a pail, and pour over it just enough boiling water to dissolve; set in a kettle of water; beat the whites of three eggs a very little, put it into the pail and beat until it thickens; remove from the stove and beat until cold. This is enough for two cakes.

Icing.

To the juice of one lemon add enough pulverized sugar so it will not run.

PIES.

Puff Pastry.

ONE pound of flour, a little more for rolling pin and board; half a pound of lard; the same of butter. Cut the lard and butter in the sifted flour and mix with ice water to roll easily. Do not knead it and use the hands in mixing as little as possible.

Plain Pastry for One Pie.

One large cup of sifted flour, one salt-spoon of Dr. Price's baking powder, also one of salt, one-half cup of lard or butter. Sift the baking powder and salt into the flour, work in the butter or lard, and mix stiff with very cold water; spread with butter, turn it over half, divide in two and use.

Apple Pie.

Line a dish with pastry, pare tart, juicy apples, slice and lay in rows on the bottom crust; sprink'e one cup of sugar and a little nutmeg or cinnamon and small bits of butter; wet the edges of the bottom crust and put on the top crust, pressing the two together with the palm of the hand.

Lemon Pie.

One and one-half cups of sugar, same quantity of water; two tablespoonfuls of Duryea's corn starch, one egg, juice and rind of one lemon.

Lemon Méringue Pie.

One and one-half coffee cups of sugar, grated rind and juice of one lemon, five eggs, whites of three reserved for méringue, two good tablespoonfuls of Duryea's corn starch, three-fourths of a cup of hot water, a pinch of salt. Beat flour, sugar, and eggs together, add water to lemon juice and stir with the flour, etc. Make the méringue with the whites of three eggs and two tablespoonfuls of sugar.

Pumpkin Pie.

One quart of milk, two teacupfuls of strained, boiled pumpkin, a little salt, one cup of sugar, three eggs, one teaspoonful of ginger and one of cinnamon. Bake in a hot oven.

Cream Pie.

Scald two cups of milk and one cup of sugar; piece of butter the size of walnut; add to this a small half-cup of flour dissolved in a little milk, a very little salt, and the yolks of two well-beaten eggs. Flavor with vanilla, and when as thick as cream, put into the crust which has been baked first, and brown in the oven.

Pie-plant Pie.

Two cups sliced pie-plant, one large cup of sugar, one tablespoonful of flour.

Cocoanut Pie.

One and one-half cups of cocoanut, one quart of sweet milk, three eggs, reserving the white of one egg, one-half a cup of sugar and bake; make a méringue of the white of one egg and a little powdered sugar, and brown in the oven.

Custard Pie.

One pint of milk, pinch of salt, three eggs, three and one-half tablespoonfuls of sugar, flavor, and bake slowly.

Méringue Custard Pie.

Yolks of four eggs, sugar to taste, pinch of salt, and milk to fill a medium-sized plate; grate a little nutmeg on top. Bake slowly. Beat the whites of four eggs with two tablespoonfuls of sugar, spread over the top, and lightly brown in the oven.

Mince Meat.

One pint of finely-chopped meat, three pints of chopped apple, one large cup of molasses, one large cup of boiled cider, one large cup of sugar, one-half pint of the liquor which the meat has been cooked in, one teaspoonful each of salt, cloves, and cinnamon. Half a pound of finely-chopped suet. Simmer slowly until all is well mixed, and add a little water if not moist enough when ready to use.

PUDDINGS.

"If you would make a pudding wi' thinking of the batter it 'ud be easy getting dinner."

General Directions.

IF you intend to boil a pudding, be sure and have the water boiling before you put the pudding in. A tin pudding boiler, with a hollowed centre, is preferable to a cloth bag—it should be well buttered before the pudding is turned in, to prevent it from breaking when turned out. If a bag is used, make it of thick twilled cotton, wet it in cold water, and flour well before using, allowing room for the pudding to swell. Puddings in which berries are used require more flour than those without, and the fruit should be added the last thing. In baking, fruit, rice, corn starch, and bread puddings require a moderate oven; custard and batter puddings should be put in the oven as soon as mixed, and be baked quickly.

Graham Pudding.

One cup each of molasses and sweet milk, two cups graham flour, one egg, a little salt and nutmeg, one-half teaspoonful of soda, one cup full of chopped raisins, dredged with flour. Steam three hours.

Steamed Pudding.

One cup of molasses and one cup of milk, one half cup of butter and three eggs, three cups of flour, one teaspoonful of soda, one cup of raisins, a little cinnamon, cloves, and nutmeg. Steam two hours, and eat with sauce or sweetened whipped cream.

Cottage Pudding.

One cup of sugar, one tablespoonful of butter, one egg, small cup of milk, two teaspoonfuls Dr. Price's baking powder, and flour to make like soft cake.

Indian Pudding.

Scald one quart of sweet milk, into it stir five rounded tablespoonfuls of Indian meal, one teacupful of brown sugar, or five tablespoonfuls of molasses, one teaspoonful of ginger, and a little salt; put in a moderate oven to bake; in half an hour stir in one cup of cold, rich milk, and bake two hours; add a cup of stoned raisins when you do the milk, if desired; eat with cream.

Rice Pudding.

One cup of rice, nine cups of rich milk, one cup of sugar, a little salt, and cinnamon; stir occasionally, and bake in a moderate oven till the consistency of cream.

Queen of Puddings.

One pint of bread crumbs, one quart of milk, one cup of sugar, yolks of four eggs, butter the size of an egg, and grated rind of one lemon. Bake in buttered dish two-thirds full. When done spread over the top, while hot, a layer of jelly or preserves (Cairns' Scotch Home-made), and cover with a meringue made of the whites of the four eggs and a cup of sugar. Put back in the oven to brown lightly.

Apple Pudding.

Chop bread crumbs very fine, chop the same quantity of sour apples, that have been pared and cored; butter a deep pudding dish, and put a layer of the bread crumbs in the bottom, with little pieces of butter, then a layer of apples, a little salt, sugar, and cinnamon; add apples and bread crumbs till the dish is nearly full. Room must be left for the bread to swell; top layer must be bread crumbs. Pour in hot water till you can see it, and bake one or two hours, or till it is brown. Serve with sauce.

White Steamed Pudding.

One cup of sugar, one egg, two tablespoonfuls of melted butter, one cup of sweet milk, two cups of flour, one heaping teaspoonful of Dr. Price's baking powder. Steam one hour and eat with sauce.

Steamed Cabinet Pudding.

One cup of stale bread, one cup of milk, one egg, one saltspoonful of salt, one-quarter of a cup of fruit, one teaspoonful of butter, one tablespoonful of sugar. Butter a mould, break the bread into small pieces, clean and cut up the fruit. Make a custard by beating the egg and adding the sugar, milk, and salt. Place the bread and fruit in alternate layers in the mould, pour on the custard, and steam half an hour. Serve with sauce.

Suet Pudding.

One cup of suet chopped, one cup of molasses, two cups of chopped raisins, one cup of sweet milk, four cups of flour, one egg, one teaspoonful of salt. Boil or steam three hours.

PUDDINGS.

English Plum Pudding.

One-half pound each of bread crumbs, raisins, and currants, one-fourth pound each of citron and suet, one coffee-cup of sugar, teaspoonful of cinnamon, ginger, and nutmeg, one pint of sweet milk, six eggs well beaten, stirred in the milk, and added last, with one-half cup of coffee, or any desired flavoring. Serve with rich sauce.

Roly-Poly.

Take good soda biscuit crust, roll one-half inch thick, and spread with any kind of fruit, fresh, preserved, or dried. Roll over and over, fastening the ends, and steam one hour and a half. Serve with cream, sugar, or sauce. Soak the dried fruit in water before cooking.

Cocoanut Pudding.

To one grated cocoanut, pour a quart of boiling milk; when cool, add six well-beaten eggs, one coffee-cup of sugar, one tablespoonful of butter (put in the milk while hot), two teaspoonfuls of rose water and a little salt. Line your dish with nice paste and bake.

Batter Pudding.

Four eggs well beaten, eight tablespoonfuls of flour stirred in carefully, one quart of milk added slowly, and a pinch of salt. Bake one-half hour and serve with sauce.

Minute Pudding.

One quart of milk, six tablespoonfuls of flour, one-half cup of sugar, salt, spoon of salt, and one egg. Stir flour, sugar and salt in a little of the cold milk. Heat the remainder of the milk, and when at boiling point stir in the flour. Cook three minutes, and stir in the beaten egg as you take it off the stove. To be eaten with rich milk.

Boiled Lemon Pudding.

Two cups of dry bread crumbs, one cup of chopped beef suet, four tablespoonfuls of flour, two heaping teaspoonfuls of Dr. Price's cream baking powder, half a cup of sugar, one large lemon, all the juice and half the peel, four eggs whipped light, one large cup of milk. Soak the bread-crumbs in the milk; add the suet; beat the eggs and sugar together, and beat in the soaked bread. To this add the lemon, lastly the flour, beating only enough to mix. Boil three hours in a buttered mould, and eat with hot sauce.

Peach Pudding.

Twelve ripe peaches, pared, stoned, and cut in halves, three eggs and whites of two more, one-half cup of powdered sugar, two tablespoonfuls of Duryea's corn starch wet in cold milk, one tablespoonful of melted butter, one pint of milk. Scald the milk, stir in the corn starch, and when it begins to thicken take from the fire and put in the butter; when cool whip in the beaten yolks till all are very light. Put in a thick layer of the peaches, pour the cream over them, bake in a quick oven ten minutes, and spread with a meringue made of the five whites whipped stiff with a little powdered sugar. Shut the oven door till this is firm. Eat with cold cream.

Fig Pudding.

One-half cup of butter put on the stove till melted, one cup of sugar, one-half a nutmeg, one pint fine bread crumbs, four eggs well beaten ; mix them well together, then add the butter and half a pound of figs cut fine; steam three hours.

Strawberry Short-Cake.

Make a fine baking powder biscuit crust, and separate in three pieces, roll out about half an inch thick. As you spread the crust in the pans spread butter on the top of the first, then lay the second on and spread also, then put on the last crust, put in the oven and bake quickly. When done separate the crusts carefully, butter each again and spread thick with crushed berries with plenty of sugar. Serve with or without cream.

PUDDING SAUCES.

Foam Sauce.

One teacup of sugar, two-thirds of a cup of butter, one teaspoonful of flour, beat smooth, place over the fire and add three gills of boiling water; a little lemon juice, vanilla, or orange adds to the sauce.

Fairy Butter.

One cup of white sugar, one-half cup of butter, the white of one egg. Beat all together till light and creamy. Favor with nutmeg.

Cream Sauce.

One cup of powdered sugar, one egg, two cupfuls of whipped cream; beat the white of the egg to a stiff froth, add the yolk and sugar and beat well; flavor and add cream the last of all.

Sour Sauce.

One cupful of sugar and two tablespoonfuls of butter rubbed to a cream, one-half cup of vinegar, one egg well beaten ; add one-half cup of hot water, stirring all the time.

Pudding Sauce.

One cup of sugar, one egg, white and yolk beaten separately, stir three tablespoonfuls of boiling milk in just before serving, flavor with vanilla.

Lemon Sauce.

One large cup of sugar, nearly half cup of butter, one egg, one lemon, all the juice and half the grated peel, half a teaspoonful of nutmeg, three tablespoonfuls boiling water. Cream the butter and sugar, and beat in the egg whipped light, then the lemons and nutmeg. Beat ten minutes and add slowly the boiling water. Put in a tin pail and set in the uncovered top of the tea-kettle, kept boiling, stir the sauce and let get very hot, but not boil.

Hard Sauce.

Stir to a cream one cup of butter and three cups of powdered sugar, juice of one lemon, and a half a teaspoonful of nutmeg. When light and creamy set on ice till ready for use.

FANCY DESSERTS.

"Trifles, light as air."

Snow Pudding.

DISSOLVE half a box of Cox's gelatine in a pint of boiling water; when nearly cool, add one cup of sugar and the juice of one lemon ; strain, add the whites of three eggs beaten to a stiff froth, beat all thoroughly, and pour into a mould. Serve with soft custard, made with the yolks of three eggs, and one-half teaspoonful of Duryea's corn starch, stirred in one pint of boiling milk.

Tapioca Cream.

Three tablespoonfuls of tapioca, soaked two hours in a pint of cold water ; scald one quart of milk, beat the yolks of three eggs, one cup of sugar, a little salt, and one teaspoonful of vanilla. Stir this in the milk, and last, the whites of the eggs, beaten stiff.

Rock Cream.

Boil one teacupful of rice in sweet milk, one-half teaspoonful of salt; pile it roughly in a dish, whip the whites of five eggs to a stiff froth, with a little sugar, flavor with vanilla, whip one teacupful of rich milk or cream. Sweeten and flavor, pile over the rice in forms of rocks; also the beaten whites ; lay on top square lumps of currant jelly or any kind of jam, keep on ice till served. Cairns' Scotch home-made jams and jellies are as good as those made at home and much more convenient.

Rice Snow.

Put to cook four tablespoonfuls of ground rice (it can be ground in any coffee-mill) in one pint of water, stir well, and cook fifteen minutes; add two teaspoonfuls of butter, a little salt, two tablespoonfuls of sugar, and a little essence of lemon. Have boiling one pint of milk, pour it over the rice, and stir well; let it boil until thick, and pour in a dish for the table. Excellent, warm or cold.

Orange Soufflé.

Four oranges sliced and sprinkled with sugar a short time before dinner, one pint of milk, three eggs, leaving out the whites of two for the frosting, small half-cup of sugar, and one teaspoonful of vanilla; make as for boiled custard, and when cold, pour over the oranges; make the whites of the two eggs into frosting, with four tablespoonfuls of sugar, pour over the top, and brown in the oven.

Orange Float.

One quart of milk, juice and pulp of two lemons, one coffee-cup of sugar; add four tablespoonfuls of Duryea's corn starch, mixed in a little cold water; let it boil fifteen minutes, stirring it; when cool, pour it over four sliced oranges. Spread over the top the beaten whites of three eggs, sweetened and flavored with vanilla; serve with cream.

Coffee Jelly.

Half a box of Cox's gelatine, half a pint of cold water, half a pint of boiling water, one cup of sugar, a stick of cinnamon, and three or four raisins. Soak the gelatine in the cold water one hour, add the hot water, sugar, etc., boil twenty minutes, and add one gill of cold coffee. Strain in moulds, and eat with whipped cream, sweetened.

Orange Jelly.

One box of Cox's gelatine, soaked one hour in one pint of cold water; add one pint of boiling water, one pound of sugar, juice of eight sour oranges; pour in moulds.

Lemon Jelly.

Two cups of sugar, one of lemon juice, one quart of boiling water, one cup of cold water, and one box of Cox's gelatine; soak gelatine in the cold water two hours, then add boiling water, sugar, and lemon juice. Strain into moulds.

Spanish Cream.

Dissolve one-third of a box of Cox's gelatine in three-fourths of a quart of milk for one hour; then put it on the stove, and, when boiling, stir in the yolks of three eggs, beaten with three-fourths of a cup of sugar. When it is boiling hot, remove from the fire, and stir in the whites, well beaten. Flavor to taste, and pour in moulds.

Lemon and Fruit Jelly.

The juice of four lemons, one-half package Cox's gelatine, three cups boiling water, one-half cup sugar. Let it stand until it partly solidifies; into this stir one-quarter of a pound of walnuts broken into halves, one-eighth of a pound of figs, and one-eighth of a pound of dates, torn into pieces. Serve with whipped cream.

Farina Jelly.

Boil three pints of milk or water; while boiling, sprinkle in slowly one-quarter of a pound or four large tablespoonfuls of Hecker's farina; continue the boiling from half an hour to an hour. When done, turn it into a jelly mould, and place it on ice or in cold water to stiffen. It thus becomes a beautiful ornament for the table, and may be eaten with rich sauce, pulverized sugar, or any condiment more pleasing to the taste. It is very delicious if sliced when cold, and fried brown.

Charlotte Russe.

One-half a box of Cox's gelatine, one cup of sugar, nearly one quart of milk, one pint of whipped cream, three eggs; dissolve gelatine in milk; when hot, add the eggs, well beaten; when nearly cold, add whipped cream; season with vanilla.

Charlotte Russe.

One pint of cream, whipped light, one-half an ounce of Cox's gelatine, dissolved in a gill of hot milk, whites of two eggs, beaten to a stiff froth, one small teacupful of powdered sugar, one small teaspoonful of vanilla, one-half a teaspoonful of almond. Mix the cream, eggs, and sugar; flavor, and beat in the gelatine last. It should be quite cold when added. Line a mould with slices of sponge cake or lady fingers, fill with the mixture, and set on the ice to cool. This is enough for two moulds.

Blanc Mange.

Four tablespoonfuls of Duryea's improved corn starch to one quart of milk; beat the corn starch thoroughly with two eggs, and add to it the milk when near boiling, with a little salt;

boil a few minutes, stirring it briskly; flavor to taste, and pour into a mould; sweeten it while cooking, or use a sauce of sugar and cream. To be eaten cold.

Chocolate Blanc Mange.

One-quarter of a pound of chocolate, one-half a box of Cox's gelatine, one quart of milk, one cup of sugar; put all in a dish, set in a kettle of boiling water, and boil one hour; when nearly cold, turn in a mould. Flavor with vanilla.

Plain Corn Starch Pudding.

One quart of milk, five tablespoonfuls of Duryea's improved corn starch, four ounces of sugar. Heat the milk and sugar to boiling; then add the improved corn starch, it having been previously well dissolved in a part of the milk, cold; boil two or three minutes, stirring it briskly; flavor to taste, and pour the pudding into moulds. When cold, turn it out, and serve with cold stewed fruit, preserves, or jellies, as a sauce.

Floating Island.

One quart of milk, four eggs, whites and yolks beaten separately, four tablespoonfuls of sugar, two teaspoonfuls of almond or vanilla. Heat the milk to scalding, beat the yolks, stir them into the sugar, and pour upon them gradually a cupful of the hot milk. Return to the saucepan and boil till it begins to thicken. When cool, flavor and pour into a glass dish; heap upon the top a méringue of the whites whipped stiff, and drop on small pieces of jelly or preserved fruit.

Baked Cup Custards.

One quart of milk, five eggs, five tablespoonfuls of sugar, nutmeg, and vanilla; scald the milk and pour upon the beaten yolks and sugar; add to this, when you have flavored it, the whites of two eggs; fill small stoneware cups, and set in a dripping-pan of boiling water. Bake until "set," cover with méringue made of the whisked whites of the three eggs and a little powdered sugar. Bake till light brown; eat cold from the cups.

Boiled Custard.

One quart of milk, yolks of five eggs, and whites of two, reserving three for the méringue, six tablespoonfuls of sugar, two teaspoonfuls of flavoring extract. Heat the milk to scalding, pour gradually on the beaten yolks and two whites, whipped light with the sugar. Return to the custard kettle, and stir until it begins to thicken. When cold, flavor; pour in a glass or china dish, whip the whites of the three eggs with a little sugar, and put on the top. Lay a preserved berry or bit of jelly on the top of the whites. Serve with cake if desired.

Prune Jelly.

One quart of Turkish prunes, two lemons, one box of Cox's gelatine, sugar to taste; soak the prunes in three pints of cold water from twelve to twenty-four hours; when fully soaked out, stew them till very tender, adding sugar, as you would for the table, before taking from the fire; soak the gelatine in one pint of cold water, turn the juice of the stewed prunes into a quart measure, and fill it up with hot water; turn this and the juice of two lemons into the soaked gelatine, and cook until it boils; stone the prunes, and put enough to fill your mould one-third full. When the jelly boils, strain it into the moulds through a coarse cloth.

IMPERIAL GRANUM.

Dessert.

The Imperial Granum, in its elementary composition, contains the medicinal and nutritive qualities in superior excellence, and there are many delicious forms in which it may be prepared for the table, the methods of preparing which we leave to the ingenuity and taste of the consumer. We give, however, receipts for preparing a most healthful and delicious dessert service, translated from the French of M. Paschal, chef de cuisine, Paris.

Crême de Thyra.

Use two heaping tablespoonfuls of Imperial Granum and one quart of milk. Dissolve the Granum in a little of the cold milk, to which add two well-beaten eggs, four tablespoonfuls of white sugar, and a very little salt; mix well together. Boil the rest of the milk, and stir in the mixture; continue boiling it slowly until a creamy appearance is observed, then remove it from the fire; flavor with lemon, vanilla, chocolate, or to the taste, and pour it hot into cups. When cold, it is ready for the table. The eggs can be omitted by using three heaping tablespoonfuls of the Imperial Granum.

Tarte d'Elysee.

Prepare the "Crême de Thyra" with same proportions and in the same manner as above directed. The quantity will be ample for two pies. Have in readiness four nicely-made, equal-sized pie crusts, baked on dinner plates (ordinary pie plates are too deep), spread the cream hot on one of them, then cover it with the other, and serve warm or cold. The crusts should be hot from the oven when the cream is spread upon them. Sift a little pulverized sugar on the top crust. If this pie is well made it will be difficult to conceive of anything more wholesome and delicious.

NOTE.—The above recipes are given for a specified quantity. Observe the same proportions for more or less.

Ice Cream.

One quart of rich milk, eight eggs, whites and yolks beaten separately and very light, four cups of sugar, three pints sweet cream, five tablespoonfuls flavoring, a pinch of salt. Heat the milk to almost boiling, beat the yolks light, add the sugar, and stir well. Pour the hot milk to this, little by little, beating all the time; put in the frothed whites, and return to the fire; boil in a double boiler. Stir the mixture till it is as thick as boiled custard; pour into a bowl to cool. When nearly cold, beat in the cream and flavoring.

Imperial Granum Ice Cream.

Dissolve two heaping tablespoonfuls of Imperial Granum and a very little salt in a teacupful of cold milk; stir this into a quart of boiling milk until the mixture assumes a creamy appearance, then remove it from the fire, and add five tablespoonfuls of white granulated sugar; stir it frequently while cooling. When cold, and just before putting it into the freezer, flavor with lemon, vanilla, chocolate, or to suit the taste. It is best without flavor for invalids. Observe the same proportions for more or less.

If, for dessert, a very rich cream is desired, stir into the above (after flavoring, and just before freezing) one pint of whipped sweet cream.

This most delicious Cream of the Creams is highly recommended for its unrivalled nutritive and sanatory excellence. It will leave no bad taste in the mouth, as is invariably the case with frozen custard, or frozen compounds of eggs, corn starch, etc.

Not only for those in health, but for invalids, and for convalescents from all forms of disease, especially fevers, it is unequalled for its soothing and nourishing qualities.

BEVERAGES.

*" Coffee, which makes the politician wise,
And see through all things with his half-shut eyes."*

Coffee.

ALLOW a heaping tablespoonful to each person and one extra; use half the white of one egg for six persons, and mix it with the coffee; then moisten thoroughly with cold water; just fifteen minutes before it is served, pour on boiling water, allowing a coffee-cupful for each person and one extra; let it boil about five minutes, stirring it when the coffee rises to the top; place on back of stove to settle, or add a tablespoonful of cold water;—

Or,

Prepare the coffee and egg as above, put the mixture into cold water in a tightly-covered vessel, and boil five minutes; or have a pot or can that fits into the tea-kettle, and steam, keeping the water in the tea-kettle boiling all the time. Java and mocha, mixed in equal quantities, make a nice-flavored coffee.

Tea.

For moderate strength, use one teaspoonful to half a pint of water; pour on boiling water, leaving the pot standing where it will be at the boiling-point, yet will not boil, for from three to five minutes, keeping tightly covered.

Chocolate.

A Famous Washington Recipe.—Break up the chocolate and place in a warm spot to melt; put in a farina kettle, and pour on boiling milk; stir while pouring in the milk, and stir constantly while cooking; let it boil some minutes, and serve with whipped cream. Use Fry's sweetened chocolate.

Cocoa.

For a breakfast cup.—Put into the cup half a teaspoonful of Fry's cocoa and a spoonful of sugar; fill up slowly with boiling water, stirring the while. Add milk or cream to suit the taste, and more sugar if required.

Communion Wine.

Three pounds of grapes, two of white sugar, three quarts of water; scald the grapes and water slowly, then mash and strain; add the sugar, boil, and seal, as for canned fruit.

A Summer Drink.

Two pounds Catawba grapes, three tablespoonfuls loaf sugar, one cup cold water. Squeeze the grapes in a coarse cloth, when you have picked them from the stems. Wring out every drop of juice, add the sugar, and when this is dissolved, the water. Surround with ice until very cold; put a lump of ice into a pitcher, pour the mixture upon it and drink at once. If not sweet enough, add more sugar.

JELLIES AND PRESERVES.

Peaches.

PARE and place them on a plate in the steamer, over boiling water, keeping them tightly covered, steam till they can be easily pierced with a fork; put them in heated cans, keeping cans in hot water until sealed. Make a syrup in the proportion of one pint of water to each pound and a half of sugar, and allowing three-quarters of a pound of sugar to each pound of fruit. Pour the hot syrup over the fruit, and seal.

Pears are put up in the same way as peaches, allowing but one-half pound of sugar for each of fruit.

Grape Preserves.

Press the pulp from the skins; put the pulps in preserving-kettle and boil them a few moments; then strain through cullender to separate the seeds; add the pulp to the skins, and weigh; allow three-fourths of a pound of sugar to one pound of fruit. Cook slowly, from one-half to three-fourths of an hour.

Currant Jelly.

To one heaping quart of fruit, put a small half-cup of water. Put fruit in preserving-kettle, and cook to pulp; then put in bag and strain, do not squeeze. To each pint of juice, allow one pound of sugar. Cook from three to eight minutes, and pour in glasses.

Crab Apple Jelly.

Remove the stems and blossoms from fruit, cut in two, and put in porcelain kettle, with water to nearly cover; cook until soft, put in a flannel bag, and drain. For each pint of juice allow one pound of sugar, boil the juice ten or fifteen minutes, skim thoroughly, heat the sugar in the oven, and add to the juice; then let it just come to a boil, and strain into glasses.

Strawberry Jam.

For every pound of fruit, three-quarters of a pound of sugar, one pint of red currant juice to every four pounds of strawberries. Boil the juice of the currants with the strawberries half an hour, stirring all the time. Add the sugar, and boil up rapidly for about twenty minutes, skimming carefully. Put in small jars.

Baked Apples.

Cut out the blossom end of sweet apples—Campfields or Pound Sweets—with a sharp penknife; wash, but do not pare them, pack in a large pudding dish, pour a cupful of water in the bottom, cover closely with another dish or pan; set in a moderate oven, and steam until tender all through. Pour the liquor over them while hot, and repeat this as they cool. Set on the ice several hours before tea, and when you are ready, transfer to a glass dish, pouring the juice over them again. Eat with powdered sugar and cream.

Should you object to the worry and trouble of putting up your own jellies, we would recommend to you Cairns' Scotch home-made jellies, jams, and marmalades, which we have tried, and find superior to anything of the kind we have ever used.

PICKLES AND RELISHES.

Sweet Cucumber Pickle.

TAKE ripe cucumbers, pare them and cut out the the seeds; cut in strips and soak in weak brine twenty-four hours; then put them in vinegar and soak twenty-four hours longer; then put them in sweetened vinegar (the same as for any sweet pickle), and cook until tender. To one and one-half quarts of vinegar, four cups of brown sugar, a tablespoonful ground cinnamon (tied in a cloth), also a few whole cloves. Put away in jars.

Sweet Pickle.

Seven pounds of fruit, three and one-half pounds sugar, one pint vinegar, two tablespoonfuls each of ground cloves and cinnamon (put in a bag); boil syrup first, pare your fruit, and cook till tender. Put in jars and pour syrup over.

Chili Sauce.

Thirty ripe tomatoes, five large onions, two large peppers, one cup of vinegar, two tablespoonfuls sugar, one of salt; chop the vegetables, add cinnamon and cloves to taste, and boil one hour or more.

Boston Tomato.

Nine pounds ripe tomatoes, four pounds dark brown sugar; boil down thick; add one teaspoonful each of cloves, cinnamon, and mace, and one quart of vinegar; boil down again until thick. Put in cans, and it is ready to serve with cold or hot meats.

Tomato Catsup.

One-half bushel tomatoes; boil till soft, and put through a sieve; one quart cider vinegar, one-half pint salt, one tablespoonful of whole cloves, one teaspoonful whole allspice, three teaspoonfuls black pepper, one red pepper, and one garlic; mix, and boil five hours. Strain and bottle while hot.

Russian Sauce.

Four tablespoonfuls grated horseradish, two tablespoonfuls made mustard, one tablespoonful sugar, salt-spoonful of salt, and vinegar enough to cover. Will keep for months if well corked.

Spiced Grapes.

Six pounds of fruit, four pounds of sugar, one-half pint vinegar, one teaspoonful each of ground cloves, mace, cinnamon, and allspice, one-half teaspoonful ginger; seed grapes as for preserves; boil all together one hour.

Pickled Peaches.

Rub the fur off with coarse cloth, and prick each peach with a fork; heat in just enough water to cover them until they lmost boil. Take them out, and add to the water sugar in the following proportions: For every seven pounds of fruit, three pounds of sugar; boil fifteen minutes; skim, and add three pints of vinegar, one tablespoonful each of allspice, mace, and cinnamon, one teaspoonful celery-seed, and one of cloves. Put the spices in thin muslin bags. Boil all together ten minutes; then put in the fruit, and boil until they can be pierced with a straw; take out the fruit with a skimmer, and spread on dishes to cool. Boil the syrup until thick, pack the peaches in glass jars, and pour this over them scalding hot.

Pears may be pickled in the same way.

Sweet Melon Pickle.

Cut the dark green rind from a watermelon, after the red, juicy part has been removed; cut white pared rind into blocks, and soak over night in one gallon of water, into which one-half teacupful salt and one ounce of alum have been dissolved; drain, and wash in fresh water. Scald one gallon of vinegar and three and a half pounds brown sugar, with one teacupful of mixed whole spices, tied in a bag; skim well; into this put the melon rind, and simmer on the back of the stove until tender.

Pickled Cucumbers.

Two ounces of cloves, two ounces allspice, four ounces mustard, twelve ounces horse-radish, five hundred cucumbers; vinegar sufficient to cover them; heat the vinegar two or three times, and pour over the cucumbers; put a plate or board over them to keep them under the vinegar.

CANDY.
"Sweets to the Sweet."

French Cream.

BREAK in a bowl the white of one or more eggs; add an equal quantity of cold water. Then stir in confectioner's sugar until stiff enough to mould into shape with the fingers.

Chocolate Cream Drops.

Take French cream and mould into cone-shaped balls. Let them harden several hours. Melt one cake of Fry's chocolate. It will soon melt by setting it in the oven; do not let it cook. Take the balls of cream on a silver fork, and cover with the melted chocolate.

Cream Candy.

Two pounds granulated sugar, one cup cold water, two tablespoonfuls of vinegar, and one of butter. Boil in small kettle, and do not stir while boiling. When it boils with large bubbles, take a little out and drip in cold water: if it snaps by biting, it is done. Have ready two well-buttered plates, and pour it out quick; do not allow it to drip; add a teaspoonful of vanilla to each plate; when cool, take it up quickly, and work it without twisting until it is dry and brittle; then cut and put on candy trays not buttered. Great care must be taken not to touch it while on the plates until you can commence to work it, or it will go back to sugar. A small piece of gum arabic dissolved improves it.

Molasses Candy.

Two cups of New Orleans molasses, one cup of sugar, one tablespoonful of vinegar, piece of butter size of hickory nut. Boil until it snaps when tried in water, cool on plate, and take it up as hot as possible to work; work it very fast; do not twist it. When dry and brittle get it as thin as possible and cut.

Molasses Taffy.

One cup of molasses, one cup of sugar, a piece of butter the size of an egg. Boil hard and test in cold water; when brittle pour into thin cakes on buttered tins; as it cools mark in squares with the back of a knife.

Peanut Taffy.

One quart peanuts shelled and pounded fine, one pound good *brown* sugar; one teaspoonful lemon juice or one-half lemon, one piece of butter size of an egg, one small teacupful of water. Put all into sugar and boil. When firm in water, stir in peanuts and *spread at once very thin* on tins oiled with olive oil.

Chocolate Caramels.

One cup of Fry's grated chocolate, one cup of molasses, one cup of brown sugar, one cup of milk, a piece of butter the size of a small egg. Put all the ingredients in a kettle to boil, adding one tablespoonful of glycerine, and boil fast. When nearly done, add the chocolate; test it by dropping into cold water, and when done pour into buttered pans. When cool, mark into blocks with the back of a knife.

Peanut Candy.

Two cups of molasses, one cup of brown sugar, one tablespoonful of butter, and one of vinegar. Having rubbed the skin from the peanuts, put them into buttered pans, and when the candy is done pour over the nuts. Cut into blocks while warm.

Butter Scotch.

One cup of brown sugar, one-half cup of water, one teaspoonful of vinegar, piece of butter the size of a walnut. Boil about twenty minutes; flavor if desired.

Pop-Corn Balls.

Two cups of molasses, one cup of brown sugar, one tablespoonful of vinegar, a piece of butter the size of a small egg. Make the candy in a large kettle; pop the corn, salt it, and sift it through the fingers, that the extra salt and unpopped kernels may drop through. (It will take four quarts or more of corn that is popped.) Then stir all the corn into the kettle that the candy will take, heap it on buttered platters or make it into balls.

Walnut Cream.

Make a ball of French cream about size of a walnut, and place a half-nut meat on either side of the ball, pressing it into the cream. Other nut creams may be made by chopping the meats fine, and working into French cream and cutting into bars.

Macaroons.

Blanch one-half pound of almonds. When dry pound them fine; beat the whites of three eggs to a stiff froth; add one-half pound of white sugar and the almonds; flavor with extract of bitter almonds; drop a small teaspoonful in a place on buttered paper; sift soft sugar over them, and bake slowly half or three-quarters of an hour.

11

SUNDRIES.

For a Burn.

COVER as soon as possible with common baking soda.

Cure for Felon.

It is claimed that felons may be cured in their early stages by frequent applications of iodine.

For Stings.

Ammonia and sweet oil in equal parts, shaken well together, will allay the irritation of mosquito and other insect stings, and neutralize their poison.

For Reducing Swellings.

Equal parts of sweet oil and iodine. Paint frequently with a camel's-hair brush.

Cold Cream for Chapped Hands.

Equal parts of mutton tallow, glycerine, and castor oil. After the tallow is tried out, which must be done with care, pour in a cup to cool. After it is thoroughly cold, scrape fine with a knife into a stirring bowl, then work the castor oil in and slowly add the glycerine, beating it into a smooth cream; perfume with oil of roses. It will cure the worst case of chapped hands, and will not irritate a child like glycerine.

For Inflammatory Rheumatism.

Equal parts of laudanum, turpentine, and sweet oil. Rub in very thoroughly.

To Remove Discoloration from Bruises.

Apply a cloth wrung out in hot water, and renew frequently. Or, apply a piece of raw beef.

Antidote to Poison.

For any poison swallow instantly a glass of cold water, with a heaping teaspoonful of common salt and one of ground mustard stirred in. This is a speedy emetic. When it has acted, swallow the whites of two raw eggs.

MARION HARLAND.

Insects.

Hot alum water, it is claimed, will destroy red and black ants, cockroaches, and all the crawling pests that infest our houses in warm weather. Take two pounds of alum, and dissolve it in three or four quarts of boiling water; let it stand on the stove till the alum is all melted, then apply while hot with a brush to every joint and crevice where you suspect there may be vermin.

To Stone Raisins.

Pour over them boiling water, and the seeds can easily be removed.

To Remove Paint.

Equal parts of ammonia and spirits of turpentine will take paint out of clothing, though it be dry and hard. Saturate the spot two or three times, and then wash it in soap-suds.

Ink and Iron Rust Stains.

Such stains can generally be removed from white cloth with oxalic acid; wash immediately.

Mildew.

Take lemon juice mixed with an equal weight of salt, powdered starch, and soft soap; rub thickly on the spots, renewing two or three times a day until the spots disappear.

To Wash White Flannel.

Dissolve borax, one tablespoonful for each three quarts of warm water. Let the goods soak in this an hour, turning over frequently. If much soiled, add a little white soap to the water, and rub with the hands. Rinse, and shake out well.

To Clean Straw Matting.

Wash with a cloth dipped in clean salt and water; then wipe dry at once.

Oil Stains.

Put magnesia over the oil spot, and place it in the sun. If this does not remove the stain, pour alcohol on the spot; then put magnesia on, and place in the sun. Repeat the process if necessary.

Grease from Marble.

Mix sal soda with two parts of quick lime in powder, moisten the mixture with soft cold water; coat the marble with this, and let it remain twelve hours. Then wash with water and a little soap.

Student Lamps.

The flame in these lamps will sometimes flicker. If the chimney is raised a trifle from the bottom of the socket, so that the draft will reach the flame, the flickering will cease.

THE SICK-ROOM.*

NEVER keep fruit, food, or drinks in the room. Not only is the appetite generally lessened for them, but the fevered atmosphere of the sick-room passes readily into the composition of food.

The food should be of the best quality, and neatly and delicately prepared.

Do not consult invalids about the meal, and, if possible, leave them alone while eating.

Make the food as attractive as possible by the use of the cleanest of napkins, the daintiest china, and brightest silver in your possession.

Do not admit many people to the room of a very sick person. Visitors with the kindest intentions in the world frequently undo all the work of the most skillful physician and nurse. Sensible people never take offense at not being allowed to enter the sick-room, especially if quiet and freedom from all excitement are the orders of the attending physician.

Have the room well ventilated. Fresh air is one of the best aids nature can have in overcoming disease. The nurse should be very careful to see that the air which has passed over the patient is not taken into her own lungs.

Perfect cleanliness, both of patient and room, is very essential. Even more in sickness than in perfect health, as in the former case every facility for the excretion of waste matter is of almost vital importance, and materially hastens recovery.

* By permission of Rome Hospital.

Scraped Beef.

Take a good piece of raw steak, lay it on a meat board, and with a knife scrape into fine bits. After removing all hard and gristly parts, put into a pan over the fire, and let it remain just long enough to become thoroughly heated through, stirring it from the bottom occasionally. Season with a little salt.

For indigestion, sprinkle cayenne pepper over the food.

Beef Tea.

Take a pound of the juicy round of beefsteak, cut into thin strips an inch long, put into a saucepan, and first cover with cold water; set over the stove where it will warm gradually. When it comes to a boil, let it boil five minutes; pour off and put in salt.

Beef Tea.

One-half pound of perfectly lean beef placed in a can or large-mouthed bottle; add one-half cup of cold water, and cork tightly. Place this on sticks in a kettle of cold water; bring to scalding-point; keep in this condition two hours, then strain and season with salt.

Beef Tea.

Take a pound of lean beefsteak, and broil it for an instant on both sides. Chop fine as for mince meat, then add a quart of water, and boil slowly for an hour and a half. Strain, let it get thoroughly cold, skim off the fat, and season with salt, pepper, and, if the doctor permits, a very little tomato catsup. A little rice boiled with the tea makes it nice, or a sprig of celery dropped in to lend a flavor. This soup is admirable food, and almost all sick persons will be found to like it.

Beef Juice.

Heat a thick steak on the gridiron over the coals, and when heated sufficiently to free the juice, squeeze it in a lemon-squeezer. Eat with small pieces of ice.

Mutton Broth.

Take a shank of lamb (break the bones well), put in a tin pail that has a tight cover; add one quart of water, and boil until the meat drops from the bones. Strain and add salt to taste. One tablespoonful of rice is nice to boil with it if the patient is able to take solid food. All broths should have the fat carefully removed.

Chicken Broth.

Pound one-half chicken until the bones are thoroughly broken; add three pints of cold water; heat slowly to boiling point; skim and let simmer three hours; salt and strain. A little tapioca or rice may be boiled with the chicken if desired.

Clam Broth.

When the patient is extremely nauseated by food, strong clam juice will frequently afford great relief. Open the clams, preserving all the juice carefully; add equal amount of water, and boil ten minutes; flavor with salt only; remove the clams and serve hot or cold as the patient prefers.

Sago Gruel.

A heaping tablespoonful of sago washed in several (slightly warm) waters; put this into a coffee-cup of water; when boiled up clear, put in half a teacup of milk; as soon as scalded, take off and add one or two tablespoonfuls of thin cream; salt to taste.

Indian Meal Gruel.

One quart of boiling water; stir in one tablespoonful of flour and two of Indian meal, wet in a little cold water. Boil thirty minutes; season with salt and strain. Use sugar and cream if desired.

Toast Water.

Slices of bread dried thoroughly and nicely browned; pour over enough boiling water to cover them; let them steep until cold, keeping closely covered; strain, sweeten to taste; put a piece of ice in a glassful.

Lemon Drink.

Place in a glass the white of one egg, one tablespoonful of granulated sugar, juice of one-half a lemon, and fill glass two-thirds full of ice (about as large as small walnuts) and cold water; shake with lemonade shaker until the glass is full. The result will form both a nourishing and appetizing beverage.

Flaxseed Lemonade.

Four tablespoonfuls of flaxseed, one quart of boiling water; let it remain in covered dish three hours. When cold, add the juice and rind of two lemons, and sweeten to taste. Take ice-cold.

Flaxseed Tea.

One-half pound each of flaxseed and rock-candy, three lemons pared and sliced, over which pour two quarts boiling water. Let it stand until very cold, and strain before drinking. Excellent for a cough.

Kumyss.

Put into a self-sealing pint bottle one tablespoonful sugar, one-sixth of a Fleischmann's compressed yeast cake, and fill the bottle to within three inches of the top with new m and seal. Let it remain in a warm place nine hours, shaking frequently, at least once an hour. Then let it stand in a cold place for three hours, when it will be ready for use.

Cough Syrup.

One ounce each of licorice root, flaxseed, slippery elm, thoroughwort, and anise seed; steep until all the strength is extracted; strain, and add one pint of molasses and one pound of white sugar; simmer to a quart.

Mustard Plasters.

A few drops of sweet oil or lard rubbed lightly over the surface of a mustard plaster will prevent it from blistering the skin.

"OUR TRADE-MARK"
Hams and Boneless Bacon

"OUR CONSTANT AIM IS TO MAKE THEM THE FINEST IN THE WORLD."

F. A. FERRIS & COMPANY.

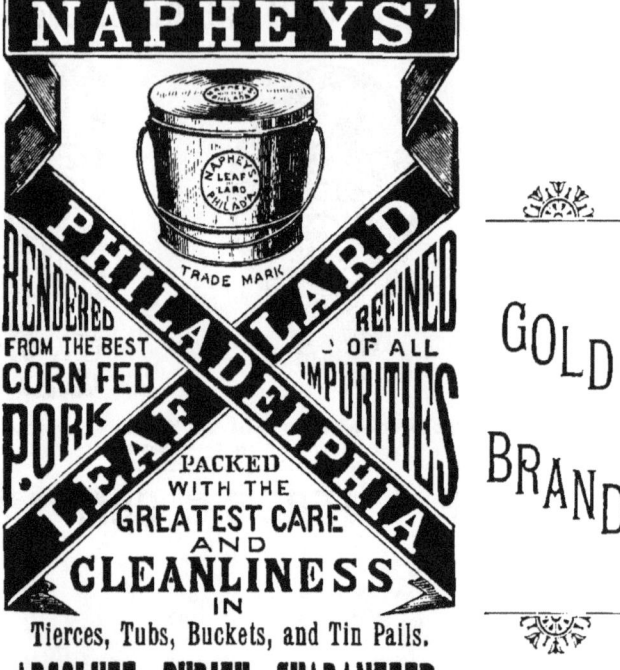

HOME-MADE

SCOTCH

PRESERVES,

JAMS,

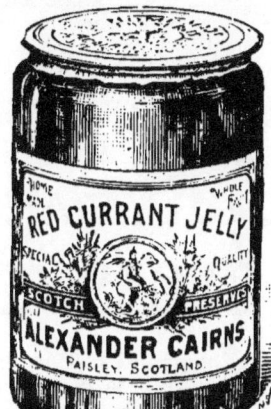

JELLIES,

AND

ORANGE

MARMALADE.

1-LB. GLASS.

2-LB. WHITE STONE.   Manufactured by   2-LB. GLASS.

ALEXANDER CAIRNS,
Paisley, Scotland.
Importing Agents: 61 HUDSON ST., NEW YORK.
FOR SALE BY ALL GROCERS.

AN UNBROKEN RECORD OF SUCCESS

DURYEA'S GLEN COVE MANUFACTURING CO.
Received the ONLY GOLD MEDAL, over all competitors, at the PARIS EXPOSITION, 1878.

DURYEA'S
SATIN GLOSS STARCH

Gives a beautiful, white, glossy, and lasting finish. No other Starch so easily used or so economical.

DURYEA'S
IMPROVED CORN STARCH

From the best selected Indian Corn, and warranted perfectly pure.

DURYEA'S STARCH,

in every instance of competition, has received the highest award. In addition to Medals, many Diplomas have been received. The following are a few of the characterizing terms of award:

At London, 1862, for quality,		"EXCEEDINGLY EXCELLENT."
At Paris, 1867,	"	"PERFECTION OF PREPARATION."
At Paris, 1878,	"	"BEST PRODUCTION OF ITS KIND."
At Centennial, 1876, for		"NOTABLE FOR ABSOLUTE PURITY."
At Brussels, 1876, for		"REMARKABLE EXCELLENCE."
At Franklin Institute, Penn.,		"FOR SUPERIOR MERIT, not alone as being the best of the kind exhibited, but as the best known to exist in the market of American production."

For Sale by Grocers Generally.

Offices: 71 and 73 Park Place, N. Y. City.

WHAT IS "REXWHEAT"?

Rexwheat is pure wheat and nothing else.

It is prepared from the finest winter wheat by our patent process which PRESERVES all the NUTRITIOUS and HEALTH-GIVING PROPERTIES of this great cereal in most appetizing and delicious form.

For MANY MONTHS it has been under CAREFUL TEST by PHYSICIANS, MOTHERS, DIETARIANS, and EPICURES with the following invariable results:

PHYSICIANS RECOMMEND IT in their private and hospital practice, MOTHERS find it the best food for their CHILDREN, who ENJOY it and THRIVE on it when REFUSING other grain foods.

DIETARIANS have discovered that it aids digestion, insures regularity of bowels, and builds up the system. Is a tonic to both body and mind.

EPICURES call it the "KING OF GRAIN FOODS."

"REXWHEAT"

makes the most delicious "mush"—hot, cold, and fried—the sweetest graham gems and brown bread, and finest muffins and griddle cakes. It is not only easily digested in all its forms, but IT POSITIVELY AIDS DIGESTION.

"Rexwheat" can be substituted for all purposes for which Cracked Wheat, Oatmeal, Graham Flour, etc., are used.

Sold only in two-pound packages. Cooking directions in each package.

The PATENT CEREALS CO., 45 Pearl St., New York.

L. A. PRICE'S
IMPERIAL OLIVE OIL.
MONOGRAM BRAND.

FEW people appreciate the WIDE difference in the flavor and richness of the various brands of Olive Oil. Some do not obtain OLIVE Oil when they order it. The MONOGRAM Brand is pure and unadulterated, rich in flavor, yet smooth and delicate. It is sold by the leading retail grocers.

PITTED OLIVES

ARE a comparative novelty in the market. They are the large QUEEN Olive, pitted, and then stuffed with a Crescent Olive in place of the usual unsightly pit. They are sold by leading retailers, and the MONOGRAM Brand is superior to others.

L. A. PRICE, Bordeaux, France.

Importing Agents:
61 HUDSON STREET, NEW YORK.

Established in 1876.

POTTED MEATS, LUNCH MEATS, BONELESS HAMS,
ROLLED OX TONGUE, GAME, CURRIED FOWL,
BONED TURKEY, BONED CHICKEN,
TRUFFLED CHICKEN LIVERS, SOUPS, PLUM PUDDING,
EXTRA QUALITY PEACHES AND PEARS, &C.

☞ No solder used **inside** the Can. **No acid** ever used in soldering the Cans.

We make no pretension to cheap prices, but **guarantee quality of every Can.**

Sold by all first-class Grocers.

RICHARDSON & ROBBINS, Dover, Delaware

The following Heads of the Great Universities and Public Food Analysts having analyzed **Dr. Price's Cream Baking Powder**, find it **the Strongest, Purest, and Healthiest**: Free from Ammonia, Free from Lime, Free from Alum, and every Drug Taint, and recommend it with **Dr. Price's Delicious Flavoring Extracts** for general family use.

Prof. R. OGDEN DOREMUS, M.D., LL.D., Bellevue Medical College, New York.
Prof. H. C. WHITE, State Chemist, University of Georgia, Athens, Georgia.
Prof. R. C. KEDZIE, Late President State Board of Health, Lansing, Mich.
Prof. H. M. SCHEFFER, Analytical Chemist, St. Louis, Mo.
Prof. CHARLES E. DWIGHT, Analytical Chemist, Wheeling, W. Va.
Prof. JAMES F. BABCOCK, State Assayer, Boston, Mass.
Dr. ELIAS A. BARTLEY, B.S., Chemist to the Dept. of Health, Brooklyn, N. Y.
Prof. CURTIS C. HOWARD, M.Sc., Starling Medical College, Columbus, Ohio.
Prof. JOHN M. ORDWAY, Mass. Institute of Technology, Boston.
Prof. R. A. WITTHAUS, A.M., M.D., University of Buffalo, N. Y.
Prof. A. H. SABIN, State Chemist, Burlington, Vt.
Prof. JOHN BOHLANDER, Jr., A.M., M.D., Professor Chemistry and Toxicology, College Medicine and Surgery, Cincinnati, O.
Profs. AUSTEN & WILBUR, Profs. Chemistry, Rutgers College, New Brunswick, N. J.

www.ingramcontent.com/pod-product-compliance
Lightning Source LLC
Chambersburg PA
CBHW020842160426
43192CB00007B/758